Paper Projects for Creative Kids of All Ages

Jim Bottomley

Paper Projects for Creative Kids of All Ages

Little, Brown and Company

BOSTON   TORONTO   LONDON

10 9 8 7 6 5 4

Library of Congress Cataloging in Publication Data

Bottomley, Jim.
    Paper projects for creative kids of all ages.

    Summary: Instructions for making a wide variety of objects from brown grocery bags and other kinds of paper.
    1. Paper work—Juvenile literature.   [1. Paper work.   2. Handicraft]   I. Title.
TT870.B656   1983   372.5′5   82-22889
ISBN 0-316-10348-9
ISBN 0-316-10349-7 (pbk.)

BB   BP

BOOK DESIGNED BY S. M. SHERMAN

Published simultaneously in Canada
by Little, Brown & Company (Canada) Limited

PRINTED IN THE UNITED STATES OF AMERICA

Acknowledgments

This book has been a long time in the making and it never would have come to pass if not for all those kids and teachers and students and friends who kept nagging me to write it. I'm thankful that they kept after me and I hope they will enjoy the results.

There are also three persons to whom I wish to express special thanks: Ann Wiseman and my little sister. Ann is an author, lecturer, artist, and friend, and she above all others kept the fires under my backside glowing. She gave me encouragement when I was down and she showed me how to "do it" when I was stuck. Then there is my sister, who propped me up financially. If it had not been for her I would have starved to death and that would have been that. Finally, Don Anzinger, an exceptional professional photographer and an extraordinary friend. It was his generous guidance, encouragement, and loaned equipment that made it all come together.

CONTENTS

Paper Projects for Creative Kids of All Ages

AT LAST! . . . A TALE SO GRIPPING . . . SO POWERFUL —
MOST PRODUCERS didn't want to get stuck with it.

THE STORY of... GLUE

STARRING

 GLUE WELLS

In an unforgettable role
and FEATURING THOSE AMAZING

TASMANIAN GLUE DOBBIES

starting *NOW* on a page near you. . . . →

Now! Meet that great team of Glue Wells and the Dobbies.

The Glue 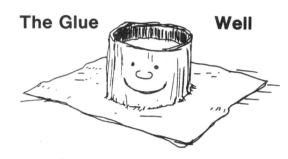 **Well**

and the Tasmanian Glue Dobbie

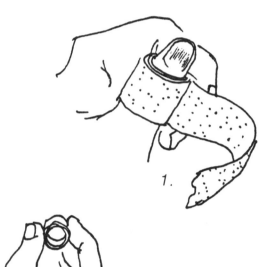

1.

2.

3.

They let you put it where you want it.

GLUE WELLS are made from strips of paper (grocery bag paper works fine).

Roll the strip around your thumb to make a tube. Glue the end so it won't unwind. Then glue the tube to a piece of paper or cardboard for a base.

Be sure to let the glue dry before you fill the well with glue and start to use it.

GLUE DOBBIES come folded up — so you have to bend them into the proper operating shape.

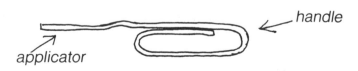

applicator

handle

Public Secret Number 63987

The secret to make glue stick quick is. . . .

DON'T USE VERY MUCH

AND SQUEEZE.

Like love and marriage, the squeezing does a lot to make it stick. Squeezing forces the adhesive into the fibers of the paper, and it also drives the water out. Glued joints will not hold if they are wet — that's one more reason to use just a thin film of glue. AND SQUEEZE.

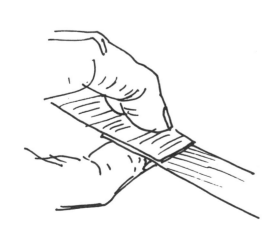

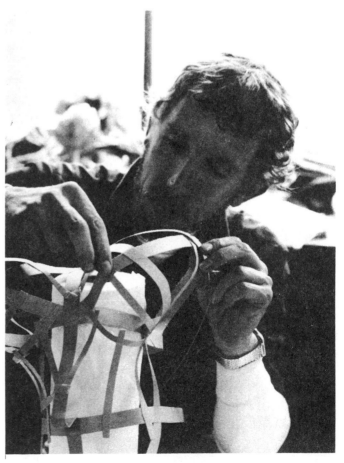

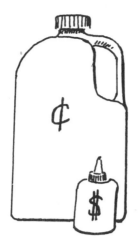

Choosing the Best Glue

You can keep thin glue a long time in old cottage cheese containers. If you cut a hole in the lid, you can leave the brush in so you don't have to clean up after every work session.

I hate to say it . . . but Elmer's seems to be the best. Try not to buy it in those little bottles with the trick caps. Buy it in gallons if you can: The savings are huge. Go in with a friend or two if you can't afford a gallon by yourself. Bigger bottles are much better buys.

STORING AND DISPENSING

I keep my working supply in the kind of plastic bottles that hair care products come in. You can use plastic catsup bottles —but they aren't as flexible. The long spouts make it easy to fill the glue wells, and if the hole is too small, just snip it off till you get it the size you want.

Don't worry about sealing the bottles. With a small hole, it would take months to dry out.

THIN GLUE

For some projects you will need to thin your glue with water. The ratio I generally use is . . . 1 thing of water to 3 things of glue — you pick the thing.

PROBLEMS TO AVOID

Watch out for the thin glue that some school supply outfits sell. The money the school saves is not worth the frustrations that kids get trying to work with poor-quality materials.

Don't use thin glue for regular projects. Use the glue straight, but in small amounts.

STAPLES seem like a fast easy answer, but in the long run glue will work better. If you do it right, glue works fast and you can make your surfaces smooth and clean without metal lumps that will eventually rust.

PASTE is too slow to dry and makes for glumpy projects.

MODEL CEMENT is not good, for paper and cardboard. It's difficult to use and to finish.

RUBBER CEMENT is fine for graphic arts projects but not for constructions. It will dry out eventually, and the project will fall apart. Also, you can't sand or paint it.

TOOLS

First-Line Tools

1. Good scissors
2. Glue Well and the Glue Dobbie (see page 10)
3. Pencils
4. Plastic bottle to store and dispense glue
5. Toenail scissors

   Toenail scissors look a lot like cuticle scissors; they have the same curved blades, but they are much sturdier. They are designed to cut tough old toenails, so they are fine for paper and even cardboard. If you plan to do much cardboard construction, you really should get a pair.

6. Masking tape for temporary holding
7. Metal-edged ruler (for cutting against)
8. X-acto knife
9. Sandpaper in various grades
10. Plastic dish with a cover for storing thin glue and brush

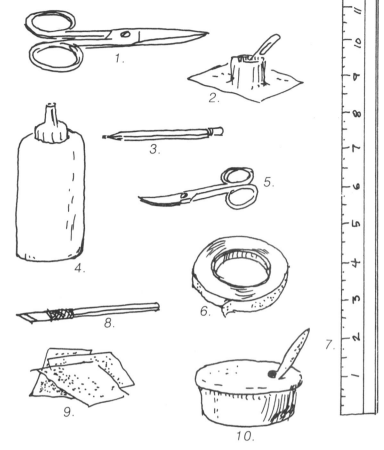

Advanced Tools

1. Tin snips for cutting heavy cardboard
2. Drafting compass
3. Paper punch
4. Plastic clothespins make great clamps.
5. All-metal straightedge, expensive but indestructible
6. Plastic triangle
7. Stone to sharpen X-acto blades
8. Beam compass for big circles

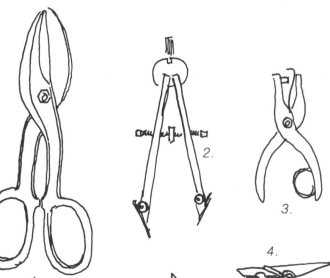

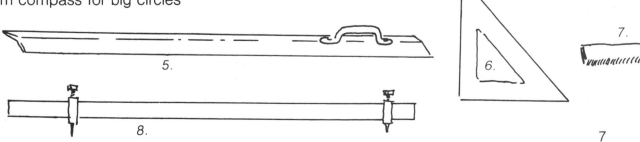

GROCERY BAG PAPER*

A GREAT SOURCE OF GOOD CHEAP RAW MATERIAL

The All-American Grocery Bag

1. Start by tearing open the glued seam on the back panel. Tear it right to the bottom.
2. Tear around the bottom edge to remove the whole bottom panel.
3. This will leave you with a good-sized piece of brown paper. The fold lines make it easy to divide it into smaller panels.

4. Tear out one of the panels and fold it double (the long way), then fold it again to make it four layers thick.

5. Next, tear right down the middle of the four layers — then tear, the remaining folds to give you eight strips of 'about the same length and width.

These are the torn GBP* strips referred to so often in the projects that follow.

* GBP Grocery bag paper

YOU NEED TO KNOW ABOUT
GRAIN

GRAIN

To work with cardboard, you must know how to find the grain direction. The easy way to tell is to bend the cardboard. The way it bends most easily will tell you the grain direction.

Easy to bend

Grain

Not so easy

You need to think about grain whenever you are cutting out pieces that will be curved.

A good way to visualize grain is to think of a place mat made with bamboo strips and string. The bamboo is the grain and you can see its direction — and you know the mat can only be rolled one way.

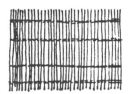

Where do you get paper and cardboard?

A good starting place is your friendly local printer. He may even have scraps that might be just what you need.

Try to avoid buying from art stores — their prices are understandably higher.

It's better to look in the Yellow Pages under "Paper" or "Cardboard." Check with box-makers and diecutters. They may have good scrap or they can tell you about local sources.

Ask for "chipboard" or "tagboard" for starters.

How Thick is Your Cardboard?

Here's an easy way to find out — with two pennies and a straightedge. If your cardboard is as thick as one penny, it's just too thick. The best weight will let two strips fit under the edge. Three strips is about as thin as you can go for most projects.

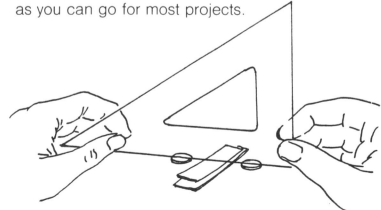

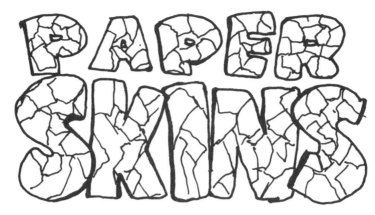

PAPER SKINS

or
Some Good Ways
to Cover Your
Framework Constructions

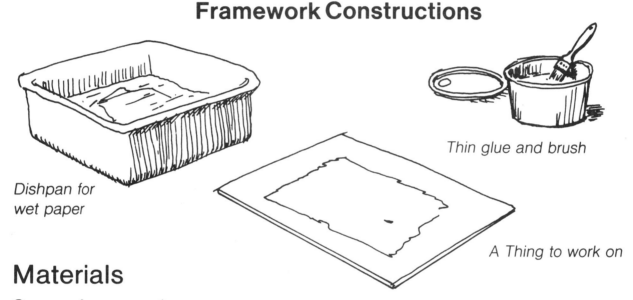

Dishpan for wet paper

Thin glue and brush

A Thing to work on

Materials

Grocery bag paper*
  Brown Grocery Bags

Tear brown grocery bags into strips and give them a good soaking in warm water, then wad them, for more softness, before you glue.

Paper towels
Both the commercial and the home kind work fine.

Tissue paper
No need to wad, but you may need to put on several layers.

***GBP**

Brown wrapping paper
Very good — test to see if it needs wadding.

Newspaper
Use only as a last resort.

A Thing to work on. I use a piece of plastic. You can use a tray or cookie sheet, a piece of wood or metal, an old shower curtain, or anything that can be washed clean and will protect the surface you're working on.

10

1. Soak the paper enough to get it wet.
2. If paper is still stiff, wad it up to soften it.

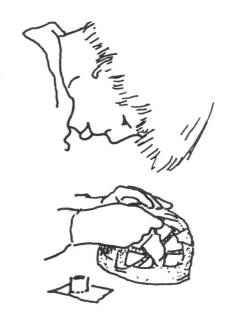

3. Spread the paper on your work thing and brush glue on both sides.

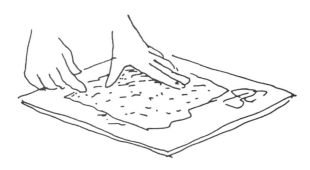

4. Tear off pieces and stick them on the framework. Some areas will take big chunks, while others will need small pieces fitted carefully in place.

Danger!

Don't overload!

If you are working on projects made of paper or cardboard strips, take special care not to collapse your structure with too much heavy wet stuff.

The best bet is to put on a few pieces, let them dry, and then add more. Once you have one full layer of skin, your structure will be pretty sturdy.

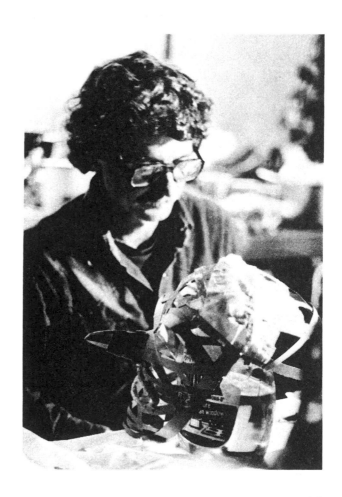

FINISHING TOUCHES

SMOOTHING Giving your project a coat of thinned glue will give it strength and improve the surface. To make it even smoother, spackle works very well. This is the stuff you use to fill cracks in the plaster at your house. It comes in a dry powder that mixes with water, or you can get it in cans all mixed and ready to go. It is white and has the consistency of thick mud. You can spread it with a stick or a knife or with your finger. Spread a coat over the surface, then wet your finger and smooth it out. You can get a very slick surface with spackle, and when it is dry you can smooth it further with ordinary sandpaper. The spackle is designed to be painted, so it gives you an excellent surface for your decoration.

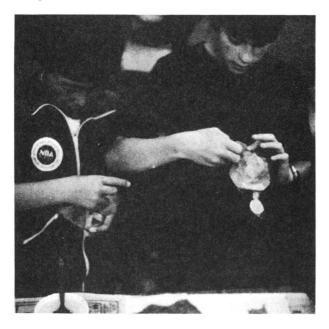

COVERING HOLES Before you can put on spackle you do need to fill the holes. Small holes can be covered with torn paper patches; larger holes can be covered with paper skins (see page 16).

BUILDING UP LOW PLACES Wads or rolls or just pieces of paper can be laid into hollows or indentations to bring up their sur-faces, and then a paper patch or skin can be laid over this to finish off the surface for spackling.

PAPIER-MÂCHÉ PULP Another good remedy for low places is any of the standard pre-mixed papier-mâchés. Mix according to directions and spread like plaster over the low spots. Give plenty of time to dry, then finish as above. You can also use the pulp to build up details like ears or auto body shapes like fenders or air scoops. It also works on human bodies to add lumps, bumps, and muscles.

SURGERY One of the great things about working with paper is the easy way that changes can be made. Just cut away the offending parts. Build up replacements and patch them in place. A good finishing job and no one will ever know.

ADD-ONS AND CHANGES Very often a few small added details make a terrific difference in the final effect. This means you should get good at small paper patches. You can add wrinkles or ribs or build up features and details in anything from a tree stump to an alligator's tail.

PAINTS Most every project calls for some kind of finish coloring. The most common answer is paint.

If your project is a part of a school program you may be a bit disappointed in what schools have to offer in the way of supplies. One of the paints that schools always seem to push is poster paint. I find it very difficult to work with. It is thick and goopy. Any fine details can just get buried with it, and on top of that it always remains water-soluble, so if you put a sweaty hand on it it comes off or transfers to everything around it.

BETTER CHOICES You can paint on paper with almost anything. I like to use acrylics, watercolors, colored marking pens, and ordinary house paints. I keep several sizes and types of waterproof black pens for drawing in things like eyes and scales and mechanical details.

HOUSE PAINTS Ordinary water-soluble house paints are great. They are easy to use, clean up with plain water, and give your work a waterproof skin when they are dry. You can find big bargains in house paint at the Goodwill Store and other thrift-type outlets. They also show up quite regularly at garage sales. A quart or a gallon will last most people quite a while. Any light color will generally do as you will want to use it just as a base and do the final coloring with something else.

OIL PAINTS Oil paints also work very well. They are great as waterproofers, but you need paint thinner for clean-up and that can be a troublesome project for youngsters. Also oil paints take longer to dry.

ACRYLICS The colors are fantastic. They work beautifully and they dry quickly. However, they are a bit costly.

WATERCOLORS For many small projects I particularly like watercolors. They have a naturalness that nothing else can match. If you learn to work with watercolors you will have gained an extraordinarily useful tool that will serve you all your life.

SPRAY PAINTS There are some terrific colors and finishes in sprays. For glossy things like racing cars or jeweled crowns they just can't be beat. However, they are a bit expensive and they do demand some special handling. Good ventilation and great care in protecting things that you don't want sprayed are just two problems.

NAIL POLISH Some of you might not have thought of it but nail polish comes in fantastic colors, has its own "built-in" brush, and is super for small things like cars and jewelry.

PENS AND MARKERS Whatever you have is worth a try, but check to see if they are waterproof before you start on an important piece of work.

CLEAR SPRAY A coating of clear spray is a very sound way to protect your project's paint job. Sprays are available in both flat and gloss. The gloss brings out a magic sparkle in your paint, and both coats will protect your project.

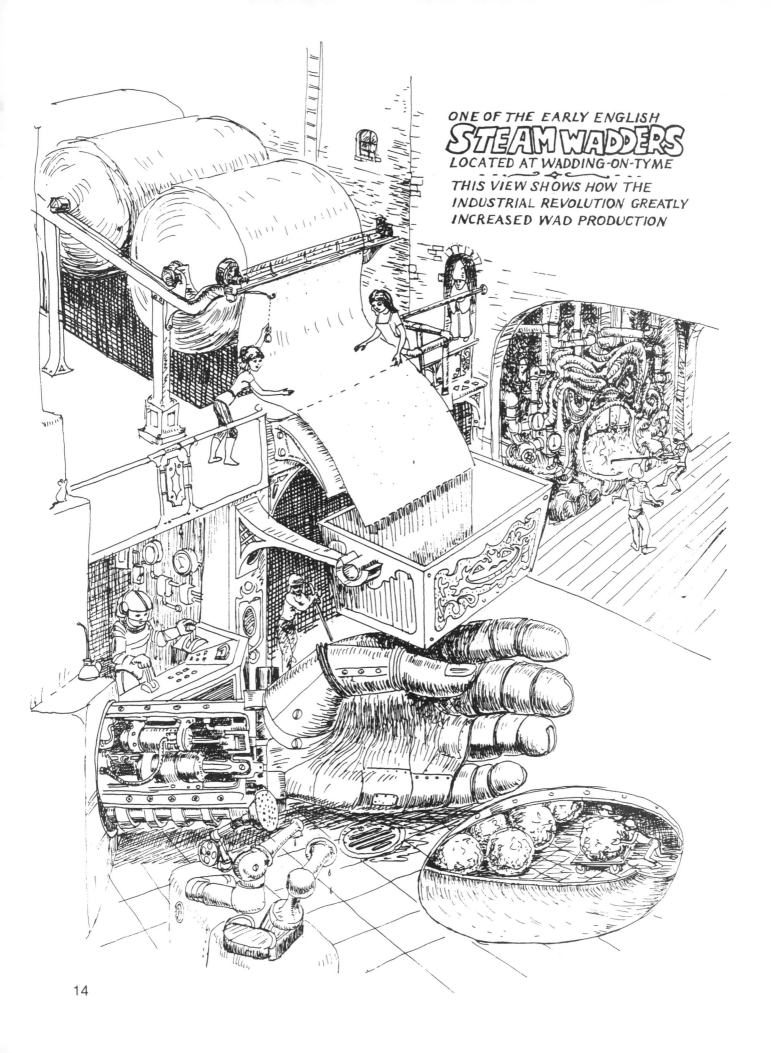

ONE OF THE EARLY ENGLISH
STEAM WADDERS
LOCATED AT WADDING-ON-TYME

THIS VIEW SHOWS HOW THE
INDUSTRIAL REVOLUTION GREATLY
INCREASED WAD PRODUCTION

14

WARNING!

Beyond this point you will find many new ideas, projects, and adventures. You are invited to visit them and look for the ones that excite you, but — before you actually start to work — we strongly suggest you come back and study the first part of the book to learn some tricks to help you succeed.

And . . . if you are interested, feel free to visit the "Teachers' Annex" (at the back of the book), where the author talks about the ideas behind this book.

Quilling

Quilling is an early American craft that gets its name from the porcupine quills that were used to roll up thin paper strips to make decorations.

The rolled, twisted, and folded strips could be combined to make intricate designs.

If you don't happen to have porcupine quills, don't give up — you can get by with cocktail toothpicks (they work just fine).

I don't use any tool to get my rolls started, and most people find that with a little practice they can make it on their own.

Your strips must be cut with the grain running the short way. This is a good example of why understanding grain is important in paper work.

Start very small. You may find it helps to wet your fingertips. Bend or crush the end to make the smallest possible roll. Keep the pressure even as you roll it between your thumb and finger.

Don't let the roll get flat. This seems to be a common problem at first. It means you aren't keeping the pressure even.

Once you do get the hang of it, your rolls will come out round and tight. The next step is to open them up a bit. When you open them up and give them some life, you can begin to see the possibilities.

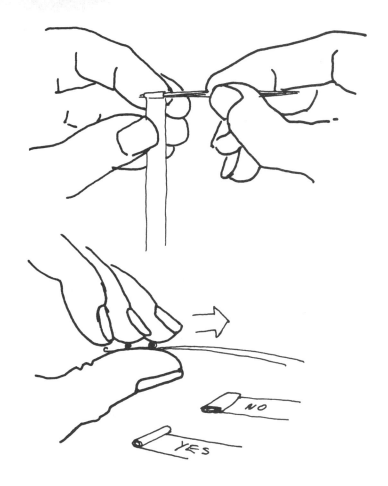

These are the three basic shapes.

This little snail is wearing a bow tie because he is going to a formal garden party.

To make his head and his antennae, cut two slits at the end of your strip. The middle part bends around and glues back to the throat — the other pieces become antennae.

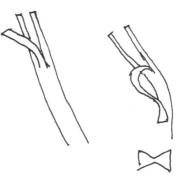

The body and the shell are made separately.

Members of the Garden Party

Duck

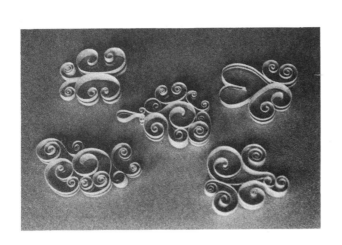

Owl

Butterfly

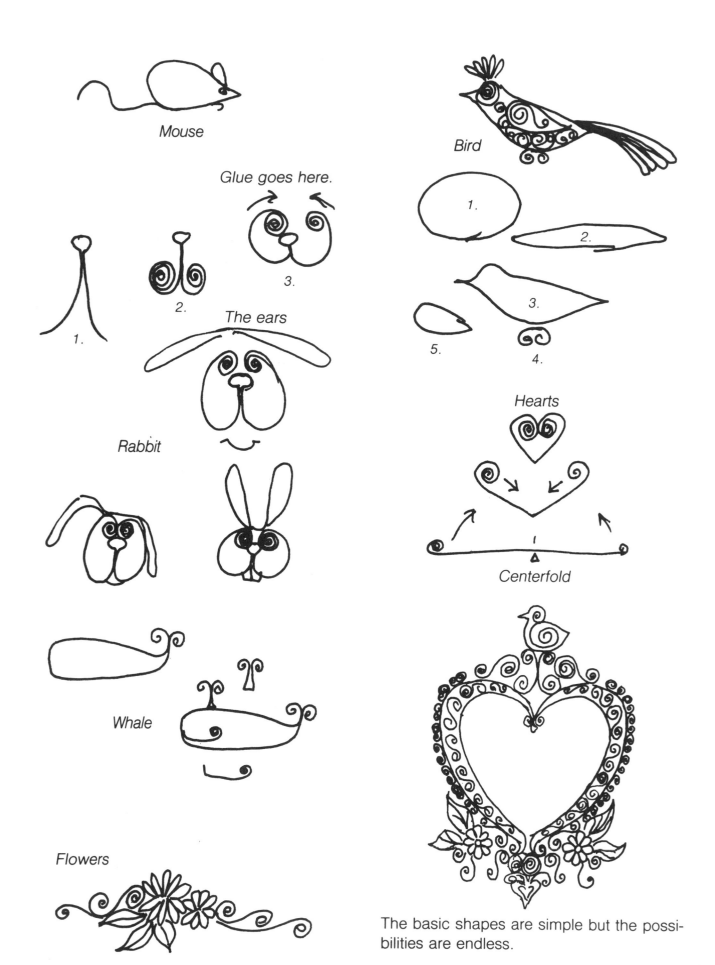

Mouse

Bird

Glue goes here.

1.

2.

3.

The ears

1.

2.

3.

4.

5.

Rabbit

Hearts

Centerfold

Whale

Flowers

The basic shapes are simple but the possibilities are endless.

18

ADDING COLOR TO YOUR QUILLING

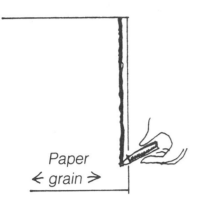

Make a line of color down the edge of your paper.

Cut off a strip with the color down the center.

You will be amazed at how much color comes from just one line.

TIPS AND TRICKS

1. Color markers work just great for stripes. Of course, you can use anything from watercolors to chalks, *but* you can't use wax crayons, as the glue won't stick to the wax.

2. Try running a color stripe down both sides of your strip. Then try different color combinations.

3. Don't overlook your local printer as a good source for colored scraps. The waste trimmings from printed sheets can make very exciting designs.

4. You can color whole sheets by dipping or brushing with paint or dye.

5. Spray paints can also be used either on the strips or on your finished pieces.

HEADBANDS AND HATS

The starting point for a lot of hats is the headband. A strip of cardboard works fine. Be sure the grain goes the short way — if your strips aren't long enough, you can glue two or more together.

You can make your own headband, but — like so many things — it works better if two people can work as a team.

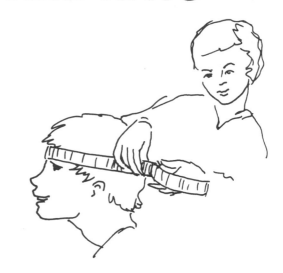

The headband goes around the head, just above the ears, and it should be a snug comfortable fit.

When you have a good fit on the head, hang onto the band so it won't slip, and have your partner put some glue under the ends.

Hold onto it or clamp it till it's dry, then have another fitting to make sure.

or wings

or antennae

Add a feather

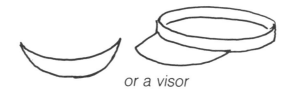

or a visor

or curls

or an Egyptian cobra

or ears

or flowers

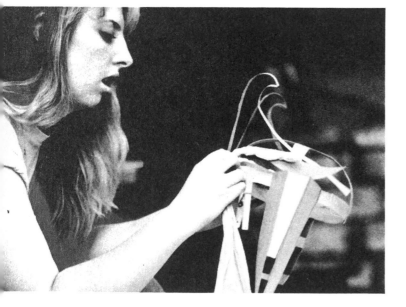

or anything you like.

This funny bird headdress is made with two tracings of your hand and two paper hinges that hold the headband together and make a beak.

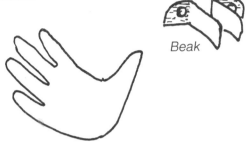

Beak

Trace your hand onto cardboard. Cut out two pieces for a beak. Glue the beaks together. Glue their tabs to your "thumb." Attach to a headband.

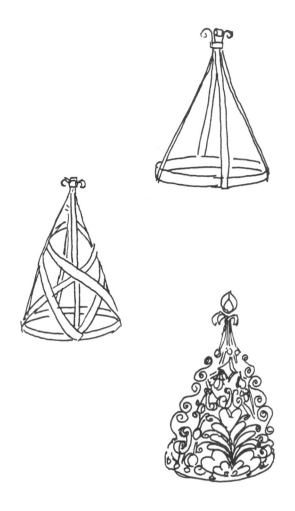

Add four long strips joined at the top with a ring. Then wrap spiral strips up the sides to make a sturdy frame and cover it with quilling and cut paper designs.

Yes, with a little encouragement teachers do get into the act.

The addition of an eye mask opens many more exciting possibilities.

BASIC HATS

This hat is quick and easy to make and fun to wear. The basic design is very simple, but you can add all kinds of decorations. You can even make it waterproof.

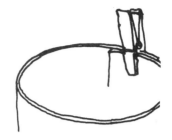

Plastic clothespins make good clamps for gluing — do you know why plastic is better than wood for this job?

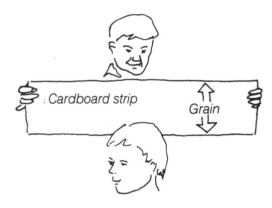

Fit the cardboard strip around the head just above the ears.

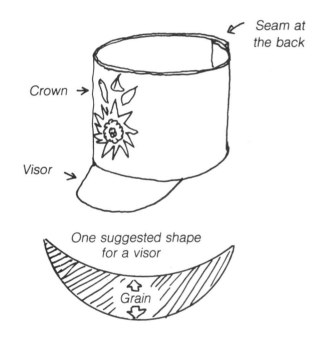

Hold it, so it doesn't slip, and work some glue under the edge. Then squeeze.

You may need to do some experimenting to get the kind of visor that you want. Cut out a cardboard crescent and tape it to the crown .to see how it looks.

The French police hat has a flat visor that fits the crown without bending.

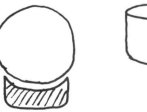

22

Once you have a visor shape you like, put some GBP* hinges along the inside edge. Give them time to dry and then start gluing them to the inside of the crown. Start with the center, then do the two ends. Finally, glue the rest of the tabs.

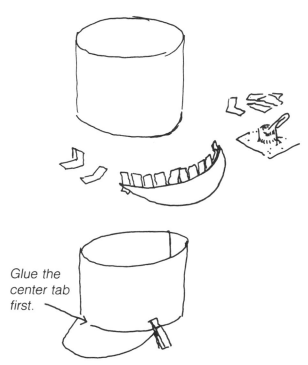

Glue the center tab first.

Then do the two corners. Hold them or clamp them until they are stuck.

To close that hole in the top — put glue on the top edge and stick a piece of cardboard on top. Then trim it to fit. When the glue is dry, you can sand the edges.

* Grocery Bag Paper

Paint (waterproof) will make your hat weather-resistant (if not weatherproof).

Colored yarn or string and buttons

Colored paper, quilled

Decorative paste-ons

Roll the edges

WITCHES' HATS

The first thing we need is a headband which will fit whichever witch it is to fit.

Then we need a big paper cone, big enough to go over the witches' eyes and ears.

Slide the headband down over the cone and line it up so you can draw a line under it. Draw the line all the way around the cone.

Leave about an inch below the line and cut off the rest of the bottom end of the cone.

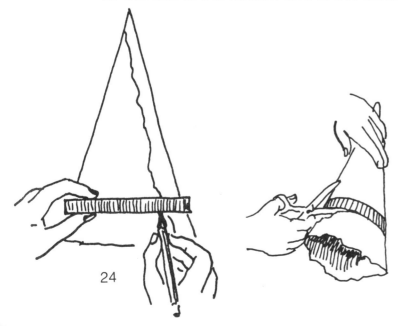

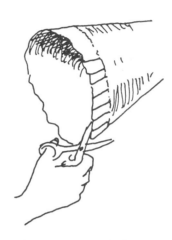

Cut a series of slits around the cone. Each slit should end at the drawn line.

Fold the tabs out and they will be ready to be glued to the underside of the brim when you have it ready.

Human heads are not round. They are rather egg-shaped but a bit flat on the small end.

So when you lay out the brim, you will need to keep that in mind.

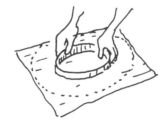

The head hole is egg-shaped but the brim is round. So you need a big piece of paper. Use the headband as a guide to draw an egg-shaped opening in the center of the brim.

Don't just cut out the hole. Instead, make a lot of pointed flaps that you fold up all around the hole. Then try it on and make changes as they are needed.

By now you've probably figured out how the two parts go together. Glue the pointy flaps to the outside of the crown and glue the other flaps to the underside of the brim.

If you don't want the pointy flaps to show — you can cover them with a hat-band — and, if you are really into neatness, you can make another brim (without the flaps), and glue it under the original brim on top of the flaps so they too are hidden.

Paints

Waterproof paints are best, not just for the weather, but for warm, moist fingers and spills. Plain old house paint is fine — the kind that you can wash up with water has obvious advantages. If you must use poster paints or the like — be sure to give them a coat of something that will protect them.

A number of experienced witch-type people have pointed out that witches' hats get pretty banged up flying around with shooting stars and banging into moonbeams — so you may want to do a little number on your finished hat just so you won't look out of place at the next witches' meeting.

Pilgrim Hats

As you can see, the pilgrims, who weren't big on imagination, just chopped off witches' hats to make their own.

Cut off the point and glue another piece over the hole and trim it when it's dry.

Historic Variations

Leave off the brim and add a scarf and you are ready to be one of Shakespeare's ladies.

Paint on a few signs and you can become Merlin the Magician.

ROUND BRIMS MAKE MANY HATS

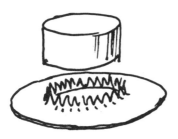

The combination of a simple headband-type crown and a round brim can be made into a great many different hats.

It's a sun hat for gardening or for a painter or for a sailor on a windjammer or you can trim the brim a bit and it's a skimmer for a dandy.

Cowboys turn up the brim for the western look.

Paul Revere liked his turned up in three places to make a tricorne.

Napoleon and other famous generals liked theirs turned up front and back.

In Italy, the decorative police have extra-wide brims that fold front and back but give a special effect.

Similar styles are popular with admirals, who like to wear them sideways.

Pirates seem to prefer the other way.

ROUND TOP CROWNS

1. Start with a fairly tall crown made from sturdy paper like grocery bag paper — make a row of cuts about one inch apart and about halfway down the crown.
2. Take one strip from the front and one from the back and join them in the middle so they form the rounded shape you want the crown to end up with.

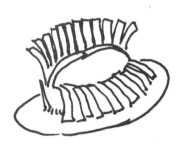

3. At this point it is a good idea to add a round piece on top of the first two strips so you will have more room for the rest of the strips to glue to the center.

4. Starting at any point, bring a strip up in a smooth curve and glue the end of it to the center piece. Take the next strip and do the same thing. Continue around the hat.

5. Some torn bits of paper coated with glue and spread over the top will help to smooth things out and also add strength.

6. Put on a hatband and shape the brim — give it some color and you're ready to go onstage or join the fashion parade.

THE BENDINIS

Little Paper People Just Waiting to Be Cut Out and Bent into Action

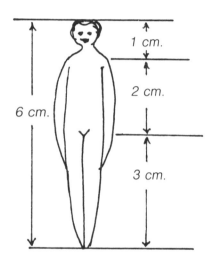

Start with a center line. Mark the crotch halfway up the center line. Add a head, legs, and a general body shape. The arms (and hands) end about halfway between the crotch and the knees.

After you have drawn and cut out your pattern, trace the outline onto stiff paper or cardboard. Fold up one of the legs to mark the inside of the legs. Then do the same with each arm.

(Of course you can make Bendinis any size — these numbers are just to give you some proportions.)

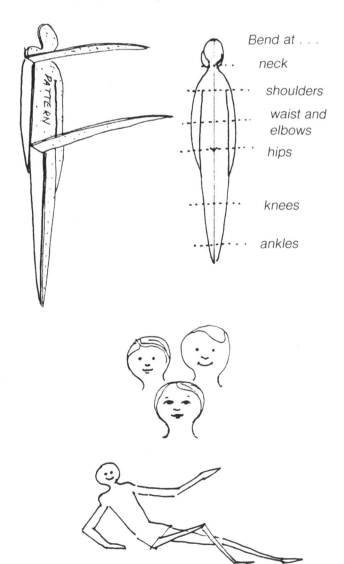

Bend at . . .

neck
shoulders
waist and elbows
hips
knees
ankles

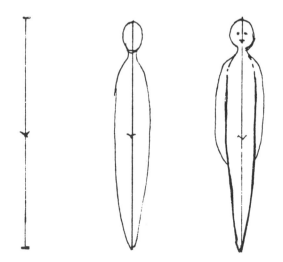

PAPER PIRATES

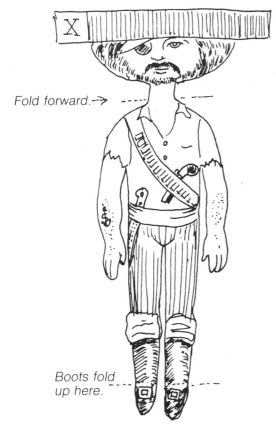

Fold forward. →

Boots fold up here.

This long neck is for you to fold him at the shoulders and at the chin to bring his head forward.

Hat brim

Fold up where the lines change.

Side view

Shows front and back glued to the crown.

Some of the fiercest and most extraordinary pirates were women. Ask your librarian to tell you about lady pirates.

Pirates like parrots.

Make two of these and glue the bodies together so the wings stand out naturally. While you are at the library, look for some parrot pictures to see how they are colored.

You can invent all sorts of tools and treasures for your pirates — and, once you have a basic body pattern, you can draw your own costumes.

COWBOYS and COWGIRLS

You can copy these patterns or make up one of your own.

A "Y" shaped crease down the front can give your cowboy a more graceful and flexible body. Some people are surprised to find paper can be shaped like this.

Wind the glue flap "X" inside the hat. Line up the ends of the hatband and glue.

Hatband is a doughnut of paper. Cut out center.

Cut the hat-brim and slip it over the hat and glue along the band.

Shape the brim in your own style. Add hair if you are making a cowgirl. Longer hairstyles can be made with a paper strip that has been cut in thin strips and curled.

Close the top of the hat by gluing a piece of paper over the hole — then trim it to fit once the glue dries.

Nowadays you can't tell cowgirls from cowboys by their outfits, and now the boys have even taken to wearing their hats in the house. So you had best be careful how you speak to a strange cowperson.

Your librarian can help you to find books that describe the many kinds of horses and which ones cowboys liked best.

BENDINI BROWNIES AND FAIRIES

More Bendinis

When I was between five and seven, I discovered that I could cut out little elves and fold their arms, legs, and bodies so they could stand, sit, or crouch or lie around all over my room. Sometimes I also hid them in secret places in our house.

I was an only child and we lived in a remote place, so these little creatures soon became great friends and playmates.

They also taught me that paper can be bent, shaped, and folded in many extraordinary ways.

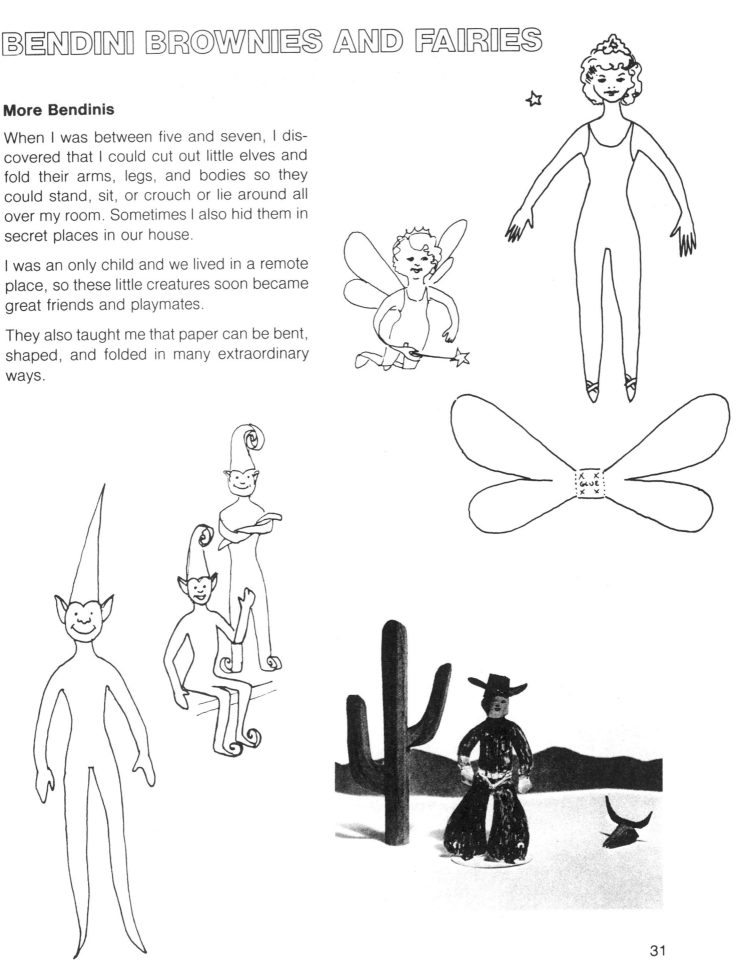

BENDINI ANIMAL FRIENDS

Dog

Monkey

Rabbit

A basic
Bendini
horse
pattern.

Cat

Cut out and fold these Bendini animals. A
touch of the magic wand will bring them to
life.

Design Your Own Heads — With Circles

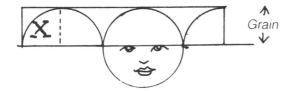

All you need for tools are something round and a straightedge.

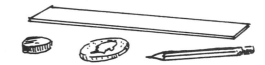

A coin or a lid can be the round thing and a strip of cardboard your straightedge.

AN EASY WAY TO DRAW SIMPLE FACES

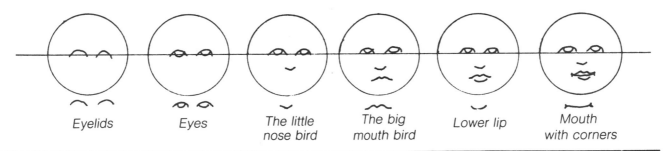

| Eyelids | Eyes | The little nose bird | The big mouth bird | Lower lip | Mouth with corners |

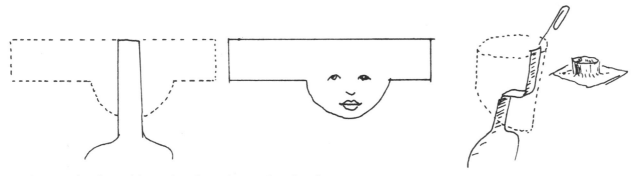

Instead of making the head on the body, just make a long strip at the neck.

Better Hands

Start with a mitten, then cut three lines to separate the fingers.

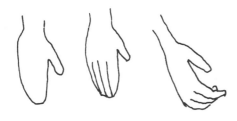

Then make the head as a unit — bend the neck strip to get a lifelike pose — then glue the head on.

Top For Your Heads

A wad of colored paper in the top of the head will improve the hair. If you don't have colored paper, make some — with watercolors.

TOY SOLDIERS

(*Pattern*)

Toy soldiers wear bright colorful uniforms. Use your imagination to make your troops exciting.

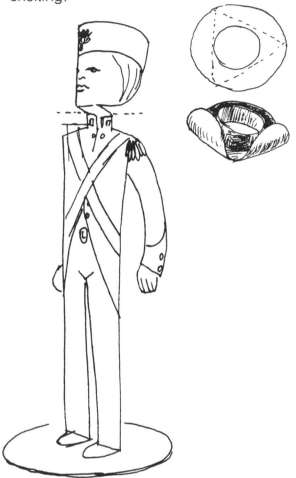

Wind the glue flap "X" inside the hat and glue in place. Fold neck forward. Arms fold back at the shoulder. Feet fold up at the cuff and get glued to a base.

If you don't like the hole in the head, glue a piece of paper over it — let it dry and then trim it to fit.

This drummer boy wears a tricorne hat, made with a round brim folded up on three sides.

Sir Bertram Bendini

Fold the glue flaps at the dotted line and shape the helmets so the flaps meet inside the face plate. The eye slits can be cut out or drawn on when dry.

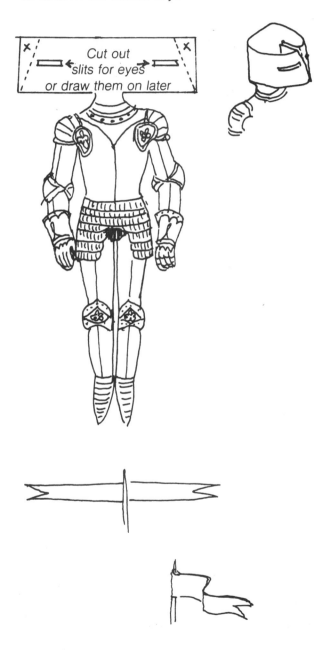

Banners and battleaxes, swords and shields are just a few of the tools knights need to slay dragons.

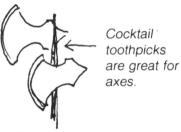

Cocktail toothpicks are great for axes.

Cut out your battleax, then sandwich the two pieces around a toothpick.

Your library is loaded with great pictures and ideas for armor, weapons, and pageantry.

You can find colored strips for pennants in magazine advertising. Cut a strip big enough to double around the pole. Be sure to put wiggles in your finished banner.

BENDINI BALLERINAS

Glue Flap

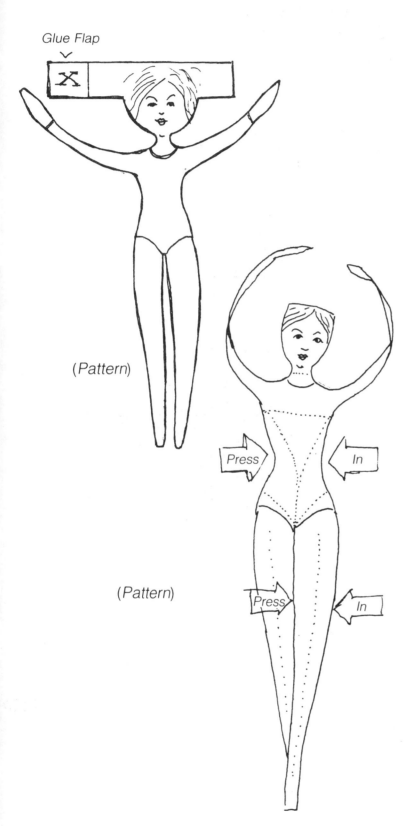

(Pattern)

(Pattern)

Give your ballerina a graceful form by bending her so the dotted lines are raised.

Don't give all your dancers the same arm positions.

With arms up you will need to add on a separate glue flap.

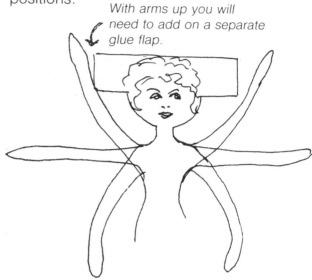

If your dancer is to perform on her toes you will need to cut reinforcing strips that glue to her feet and make a hinge that glues to the base — the combination of paper and glue becomes quite strong.

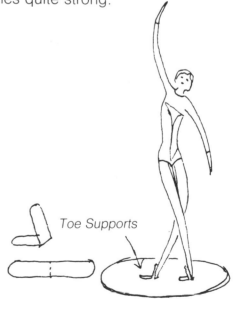

Toe Supports

REMEMBER

This is just a starter — the ones you invent will be much more fun.

Twisties

Strips of torn grocery bag paper twisted into spirals can be made into all kinds of things.

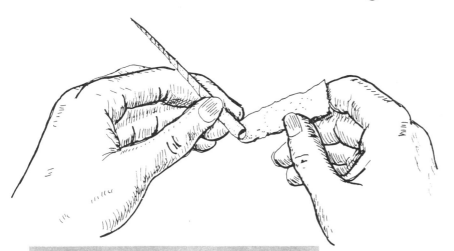

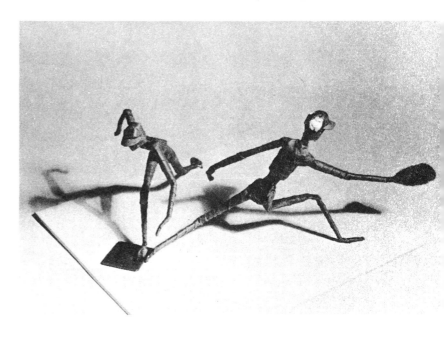

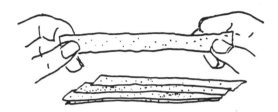

1. Start with five strips of GBP,* about this size.

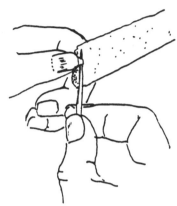

2. Roll up each strip, starting at the corner, at an angle. A round toothpick helps get them started.

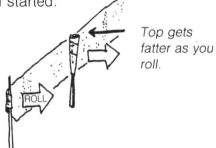

Top gets fatter as you roll.

ROLL

3. As you roll, the top gets fatter.

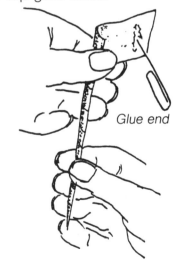

Glue end

4. Glue the ends. Don't be surprised that no two are exactly the same.
Glue end.

* GBP — Grocery Bag Paper

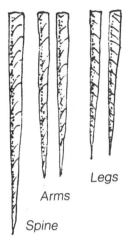

Legs

Arms

Spine

5. Sort your five cones into legs, arms, and spines.

6. Fold the arms so they can be wrapped onto the spine.

7. Wrap the arms and hips with glued strips.

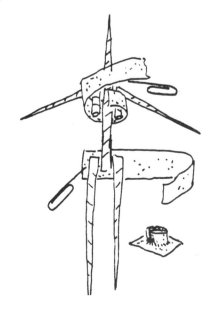

8. You should end up with something that looks like this.

9. Your twistie will start to come alive when you make a bend at each of the joints.

10. Adding short strips over the shoulders will help to make your twistie look more natural.

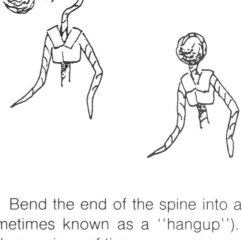

11. Bend the end of the spine into a hook (sometimes known as a "hangup"). Then wad up a piece of tissue or scrap paper and glue it into the hook to shape the head.

12. A few small glued strips around the head will give it shape and strength.

13. Hair strips are next. Then draw in features.

BISCUITS, BUNS, AND BICEPS

You can use toilet paper, tissue paper, or paper toweling or any soft paper to build up your figures and to add muscles, features, and dimensions to your twisties.

Remember if you need a right and a left, start out with two pieces of paper that are the same size.

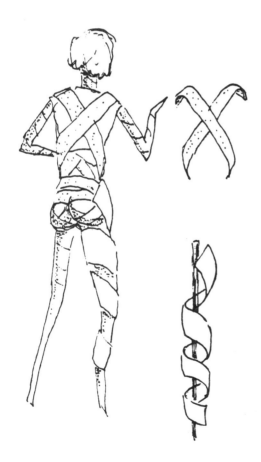

Men's bodies tend to be squarish and they can be built up with angular folded wads.

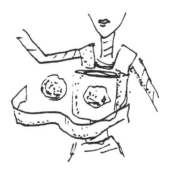

Long muscles can be made from twisted strips.

Women's bodies are generally more rounded (particularly up front), so use rounder, softer wads in the appropriate locations.

DRAWING FACES

With a Few Lines

"Keep it simple" is generally a good rule. You will find it a great help to be able to draw faces with a few lines.

Comic books and newspaper ads — particularly the fashion and cinema ads — are a great source of ideas and inspiration.

Don't Be Afraid to Trace

Tracing is one of the best ways to learn just how an artist gets the effects you like.

HANDS

These are the basic parts in the hand.

Hands are complex structures — but, if you plan to create human figures, you will have to learn to make good hands.

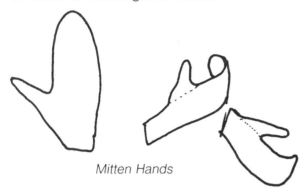

Mitten Hands

One way to study hands is to trace your hand onto a piece of light cardboard — cut it out and bend it at each of the joints — so you can shape it into a surprisingly lifelike pose.

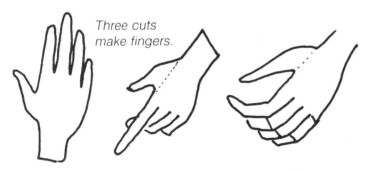

Three cuts make fingers.

Study the basic parts and start with mitten hands — then add the finger cuts.

If you take the time and effort to really understand the basic cutout hand — you will find it will be a great help anytime you want to draw or sculpt hands.

Special Note

You only have to learn to do one hand and you get the other one free.

(Just do the flip side.)

Hands from Torn Strips of Grocery Bag Paper*

Each hand takes five strips, twisted into cones.

1. Arrange them in a logical shape with the longest for the middle finger and the shortest and fattest becoming the thumb.

Wrap a gluey strip around the bottom ends of the fingers to make part of the palm.

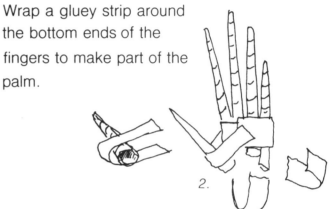

2. Wrap a short strip around the base of the thumb and glue it to the hand so the thumb points away.

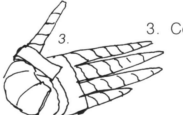

3. Complete the hand with more gluey strips.

4. Bend the base of the thumb into a more natural shape and form the fingers into a lifelike pose.

Finally, give the hand a thin brush coat of glue. For a very smooth finish you can give it a coat of spackle and sand it smooth before painting.

See Finishing Strokes (page 49).

* GBP

Building Up Features

Small bits of torn paper — coated with glue — can be molded and shaped, like papier-mâché, to define features.

Torn bits of paper can also be used for hair.

The ideas in the hat section can all be made smaller to fit your twisties.

Vinyl paste spackle can be used to form features and create a smooth-finish surface.

Little Hands & Feet

Cut out hand and foot patterns from light cardboard — then patch them onto the arms and legs. If you don't have cardboard — two layers of grocery bag paper work just fine.

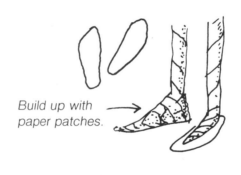

Build up with paper patches.

THE **BIG** MESSAGE

Once you have a basic frame, you can use small torn patches to build up and smooth out any shape.

The spackle gives you the final control and a great finished surface.

PAPER WADS

Once you know how to do twisties, you are ready for wads. You can build a lot of great stuff with just wads — but when you combine them with twisties you really can go wild, creating all kinds of creatures and environments.

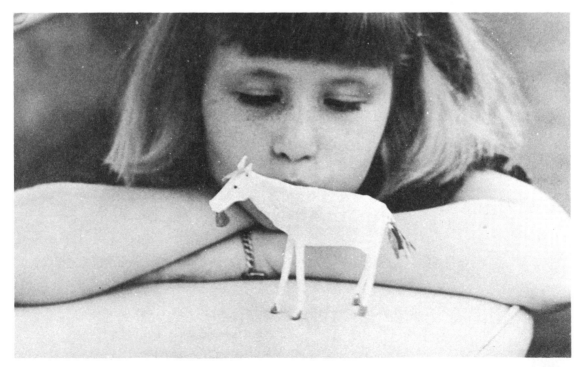

FROSTY, JR.

A little paper snowperson who can outlast the big ones

Toilet paper comes in handy square units that make it easy to measure the size of your wads.

Paper wads are made a lot like snowballs — wet the paper, then squeeze and roll into a ball.

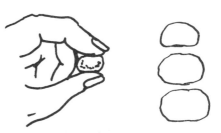

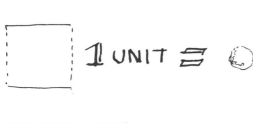

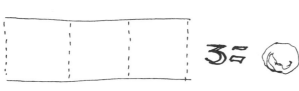

It's a good idea to squash some flattish places at the point where your snow wads will be glued together.

This is a good example of ratio and proportion.

Paper wads will generally dry overnight at room temperature.

Frosty's hat starts with a tiny paper tube — shaped around your pencil — much like your glue dobbies.

Once you have Frosty put together, on the cardboard base — and the glue is dry — you can add black dots (like coal) to make eyes and buttons and a smile.

The top and the brim are pieces glued to the crown and cut to shape.

His carrot nose is a tiny paper cone shaped around a pen or pencil. Coloring is up to you. The scarf is a bit of bright yarn or holiday ribbon.

QUICK AND EASY TURTLES

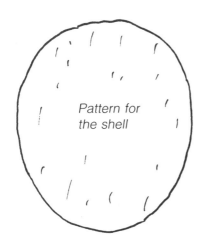

*Pattern for
the shell*

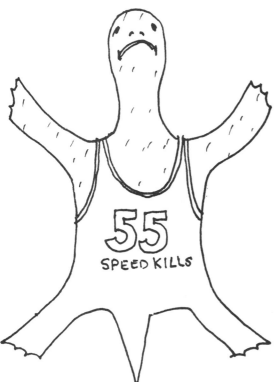

55

SPEED KILLS

*Pattern for body
(T-shirt optional)*

Cut out the two patterns from light card-board. Make a wad of toilet paper to give you a basic shape for the shell (I used 3 squares for mine). Then use thin torn strips of grocery bag paper to make the shell.

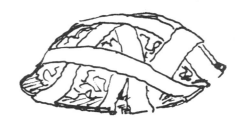

A final layer of gluey paper bits will add strength and give you a good surface for painting.

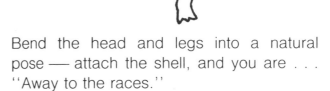

Bend the head and legs into a natural pose — attach the shell, and you are . . . ''Away to the races.''

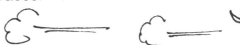

Walnut shells also work for quick turtles.

RACING TURTLES

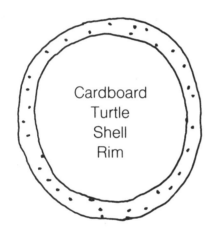

Cardboard
Turtle
Shell
Rim

Start your turtle with a cardboard circle that will become the outside edge of the shell. Build up the dome shape of the shell with torn strips of grocery bag paper glued to each other and to the rim.

Once you have the shape well defined you can finish it off with strips coated with glue.

Turtles have wrinkly legs and necks — so start by making a paper tube that fits, loosely, on a pencil — make sure the glue is dry and . . .

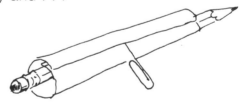

. . . then hold one end of the pencil and push the other end of the tube to squash it into a wrinkly tube.

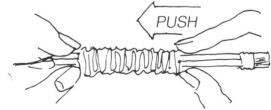

PUSH

You will need four leg tubes plus one longer tube for the head and neck.

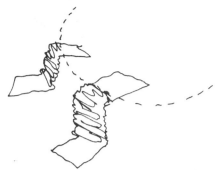

Flatten both ends of the legs. One end becomes the foot and the other glues under the edge of the shell.

You may want to do some experiments with the head — some people just fold over the end and wad it up a little. Flatten the other end and glue it to the shell (like the legs).

The tail is just a small cone.

Super Stock or
Modified Funny Turtles

Hang some flaky gear on your stock model — then add a set of "cheater slicks" made from a rolled-up strip — and mag. wheels made from two snap fasteners — wow!

WAD FROGS

OH! MY — WHAT HAS STEPPED ON MY EGG?!

Wadfrogs start with wads of wet toilet paper that have been shaped like a rubber egg that has been squashed down.

When your wad has dried (overnight) wrap it with strips of grocery bag paper. Make the first ring around the middle, then the next from end to end, and keep adding strips till all the white is covered up.

The eyes go on top up near the front (over-looking the mouth). They are made from very small wads glued on with torn strips that loop over them to make those froggish eye lumps. Use more small strips to round off the back of the eye lumps and blend them into the head.

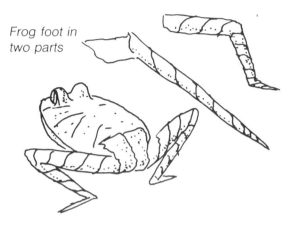

Frog foot in two parts

The legs are made from strips of torn grocery bag paper that have been wound in a tight spiral to make a sturdy tapered cone. The back legs are much bigger than the front.

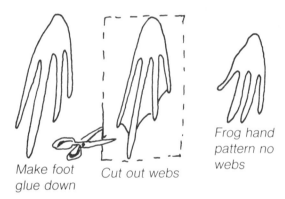

Make foot glue down

Cut out webs

Frog hand pattern no webs

The back feet are much bigger than the front. They can be cut from two or three layers of grocery bag paper glued together. Cut out the fingers and toes, then glue the feet to a larger piece of paper and trim them to make the webs.

To get a smooth slick watery frog, use spackle to cover the edges and smooth the wrinkles, then paint in frog colors and cover with clear shiny spray.

(See page 12 for Finishing Touches.)

HORSE WADS

The basic elements of this horse are two wads or spheres. I used one paper towel for each — I wet the towel, wadded it up, and let it dry overnight. (Plan Ahead.)

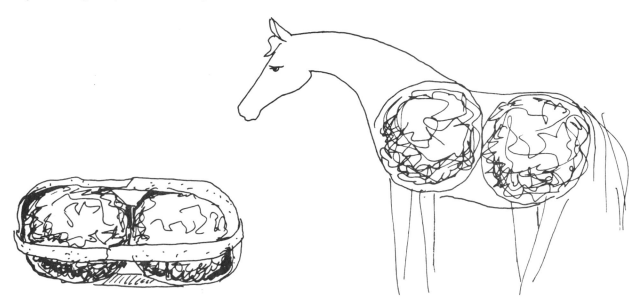

When dry, the two wads are wrapped with two strips and then the tummy can be filled out a bit with a piece of toilet paper.

The neck is two twisties made from strips about 12 cm. long and 2 cm. wide. They attach at the shoulder and on the chest.

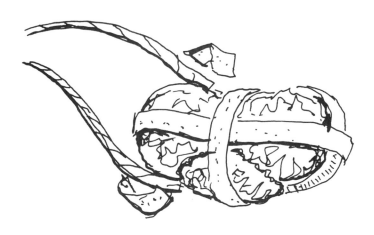

Cover the body — but not the neck — with glued strips.

Patterns

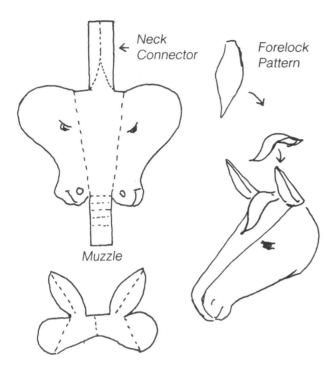

Neck Connector

Forelock Pattern

Muzzle

Trace the patterns for the head and the ears and transfer them to some light cardboard. Cut them out carefully. The dotted lines show where to crease and fold the parts.

Glue

The ear piece fits over the neck connector and two round glue flaps go inside the head.

The ears get folded forward and shaped into a lifelike pose.

The muzzle is curled around and glued inside at the mouth.

The forelock goes between the ears and glues to the top of the neck.

Fill in the space in the neck with some toilet paper, then wrap the neck with torn strips.

Your horse doesn't need a skull; just fill in the head with wads.

Basic legs are 12 cm. strips wound into 7 cm. twisties.

The front legs fit against the base of the neck at the front of the chest wad. The hind legs go at the opposite end and a bit more to the sides.

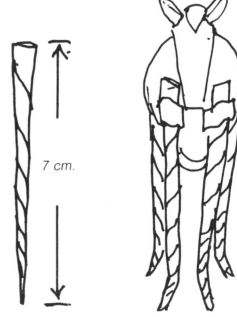

7 cm.

Down near the hooves each leg has a bend that seems like the ankle — actually it is the horse's heel.

Glue on the legs with torn patches of grocery bag paper and blend them in.

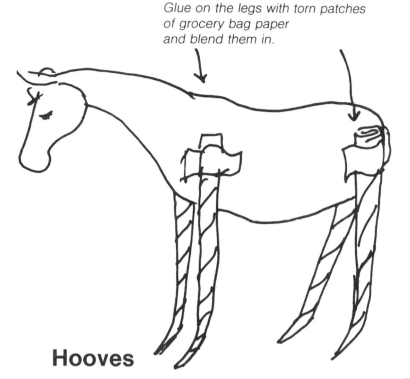

Hooves

You may have to do a bit of experimenting to get your hooves just right. I started with a pattern made from a quarter and a penny — then I cut the hooves out of light cardboard.

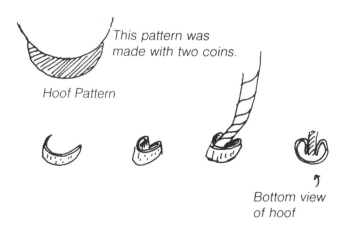

This pattern was made with two coins.

Hoof Pattern

Bottom view of hoof

Once you have the general shape, you will need to use very small torn pieces to work out the details and blend the hooves into the legs.

Water

Vinyl Paste Spackle

Finishing Touches

The body, head, and legs can be covered with small torn pieces of paper covered with glue. You can use these same patches to build up joints and other features. The trick is to make really small patches that will fit smoothly into the shape you are trying to build.

The tail and mane can be made from paper or any other kind of fiber that seems to fit. Long fibers from some types of rope or yarn work very well.

The overall finish can be made very smooth with ordinary vinyl paste spackle — that's the same stuff you use to patch walls before you paint. It is water-soluble; spread it on with your finger, then smooth it around with a finger that has been dipped in water. When it's dry you can sand it very smooth and it takes paint beautifully.

SPIDERS

The spider's body has two main parts —the front is the head and chest, and the legs are attached to the underside.

The back part is the abdomen. It is shaped very much like an egg.

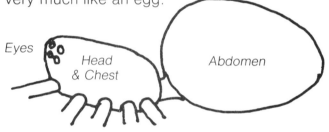

Eyes

Head & Chest

Abdomen

Legs

I made my spider by wadding up a dry paper towel and forming it into an egg shape.

Then I wrapped it with torn strips of grocery bag paper to give it a surface and to hold the shape.

I made the front part the same way, but I started with a smaller piece of paper towel.

The next part you need is a cardboard connector that will hold the two parts of the body together and also provide places to attach the legs.

It looks like a strange bug — it's made from light cardboard.

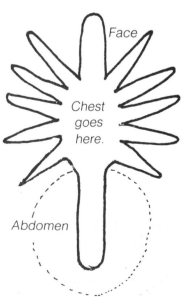

Face

Chest goes here.

Abdomen

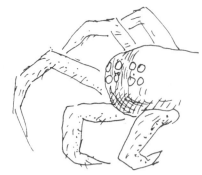

Fit it under the chest and abdomen. The long part glues under the abdomen and the short part, at the other end, bends up around the spider's head.

The spider's legs are made from twisty strips. You need to make eight that are long and two that take about a half strip.

The short legs (called "feeders") go up front, at the lunchroom — bend them where you think the joints should go.

Spiders actually have seven joints in their walking legs and six in the feeders — but you can easily get away with just three or four and only the zoologists will give you a bad time.

By now — I'm sure you have figured out that those other projections are for the eight walking legs plus the two feeding legs at the front.

Spiders normally have eight eyes — they can be drawn or painted — or — you can make very bright eyes with the heads of pins.

If you do use pins — be sure . . . NOT TO LET THE BABY PLAY WITH YOUR SPIDER.

Finishing Touches

It makes good sense to give your spider an overall coat of thin glue, particularly on the legs — so they don't come apart.

You may also want to add a coat of torn paper that has been wet with thin glue — or you may want to smooth out parts of the body with spackle.

Some spiders are quite furry and it might be fun to try flocking as a way to give them a real furry feeling. (Craft stores sell flocking.)

This is the size strip I used to make the long legs.

Here's a frisky little house pet that can add excitement to your life.

When you open the box and he starts moving his furry little legs your friends may leave suddenly.

. . . but they will be back . . .

. . . to see how you do it.

TOP SECRET

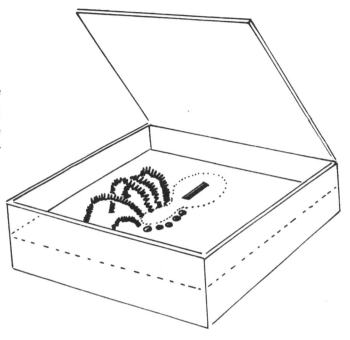

Make the spider's body in the regular way, but you won't need leg connectors. Trace the outline on a piece of cardboard. Then make ten holes for the legs. These legs are made from pipe cleaners, dyed black or brown with ink or watercolors.

You can build a box or use one you find.

The ends of the legs stick through the cardboard and you move them with your hidden hand.

Cut a slot under the abdomen and attach two grocery bag paper strips to the abdomen — slip them through the slot and glue them to the underside to hold your spider in place.

LITTLE BOFFO
THE PUPPET PRINCE

No one knew that Boffo was a real prince —they just thought he was a funny little boy. — And Boffo didn't know because he had been stolen from the royal nursery when he was no bigger than a thimble. The wicked Magician, Mistoffio, had carried him off to the enchanted forest, where he grew to little boyhood with no other children to play with.

But Boffo was not lonely — he made friends with the forest creatures and he found ways to entertain himself.

He played with a pet stick he called "Twig."

Can you imagine some of their adventures?

In the fall, when the ducks and geese swept down to rest in the forest pond, Boffo studied them with great intensity. He wondered where these beautiful, graceful creatures came from. And most of all he dreamed of flying south with them to explore exciting places far beyond the edge of the forest.

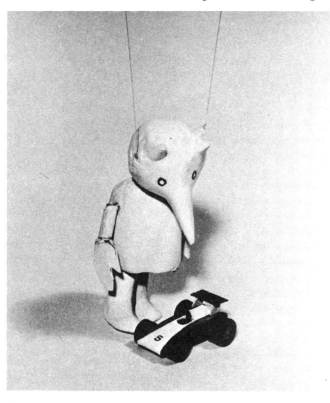

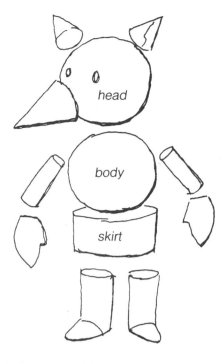

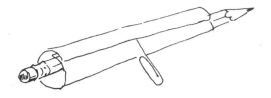

Boffo's head and body are paper wads — I use one paper towel for each part.

If you can, make the wads a day or so in advance so you won't need to use a heater to dry them.

Three paper cones make the ears and the nose cone.

Point

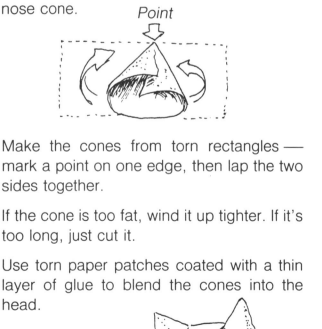

Make the cones from torn rectangles — mark a point on one edge, then lap the two sides together.

If the cone is too fat, wind it up tighter. If it's too long, just cut it.

Use torn paper patches coated with a thin layer of glue to blend the cones into the head.

His arms are tubes rolled on a pencil.

There are many ways to put Boffo's strings on. I make a loop that will give me a place on each side of the head to attach the controls.

Use the bottom of the loop to connect to the body wad.

Use more glued strips and patches to cover the body and lock in the strings.

You will soon see how those torn edges blend in and disappear.

Each hand is made like two mittens sewn together at the wrist. When they get folded together, there will be a place to hold the strings that go up the arm.

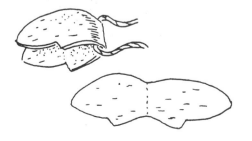

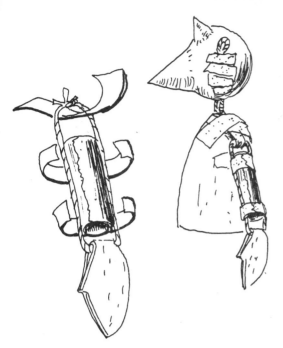

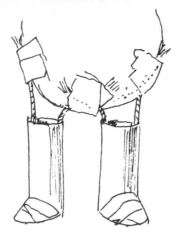

The boots can be made from tubes larger than the arms.

Toes can be built up with torn and glued paper strips that wrap around and glue under the foot.

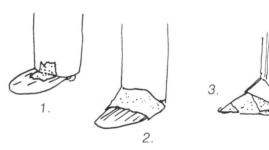

1.

2.

3.

The foot part is a teardrop-shaped piece of cardboard with the point turned up and glued to the back of the tube.

Use more paper patches to glue the leg strings to the body.

The arm and hand are attached to the shoulder with a loop of string. Try not to get glue on the places where you want the string to bend. Use torn strips of grocery bag to glue things together.

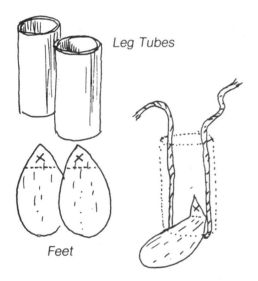

Leg Tubes

Feet

A loop of string goes around the bottom of the foot and up the inside of the tube to connect to the body.

For the best hold, untwist the ends of the strings.

His skirt is a larger ring fitted to his body wad.

The skirt ring should be just big enough to fit on the body and short enough to let the legs move freely.

60

Attach threads to the head loops and to a stick or a sturdy paper roll for your control.

Finishing Touches for Boffo

A brushing of thin glue will help to smooth out lumps and edges and makes your puppet stronger. (Don't glue or paint those strings!) See pages 12 – 13 for more ideas.

FUNNY LITTLE WITCHES
that are both Conical and Comical

Start with a cone.

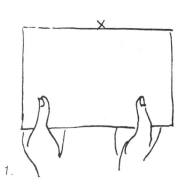

1.

2.

3.

Twist your cone

4.

Till you get the shape you want.

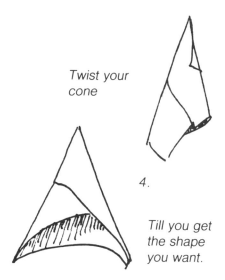

Glue

5.

6.

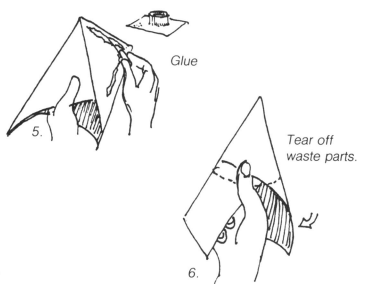

Tear off waste parts.

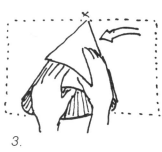

Grocery bag paper works very well for witches, but almost any paper will do. If you have black — great!

For really big witches you might start with a cardboard cone for support. Once your cone is started you can change its shape by winding or unwinding to make it thinner or fatter.

When you get the shape you want, glue the outside flap and tear away the part below the dotted line (6).

You don't need to be too neat about it. The edge of her skirt can be a bit ragged.

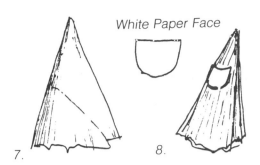

White Paper Face

13.

You can make the face parts out of grocery bag paper. But if you have some white paper, you will find the color contrast is helpful. Writing paper, typing paper, or mimeo paper is fine.

Stick the nose just under the forehead. Use those cut ends for gluing.

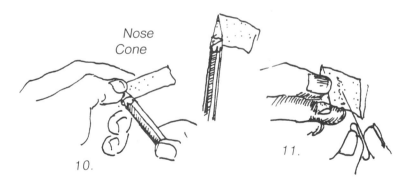

A roll of white paper for the forehead

9.

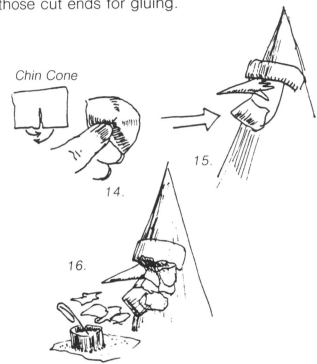

Chin Cone

14.

15.

16.

Shape the nose cone around a pencil or pen. Use a piece of torn paper so the edges will blend in. When you make the cuts on the end you will need sharp scissors. It's just too hard to tear so small.

You may have to do some experimenting with the chin. When you have it right, blend in all the parts with small torn pieces of paper.

This is a good time to draw in the eyes and mouth. Then you will begin to see your witch's personality. You may be quite surprised to find you can't make a witch exactly like anyone else's. Each witch is an individual. Just like people.

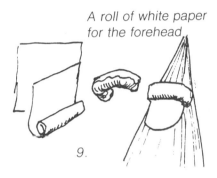

Nose Cone

10.

11.

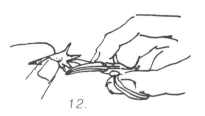

12.

Some hair and a hat will give your witch personality.

Hands You can make both hands at one cutting by folding the paper double. Cut out a "mitten" shape, then cut the three lines between the fingers. Shape the hand and fingers into a lifelike pose.

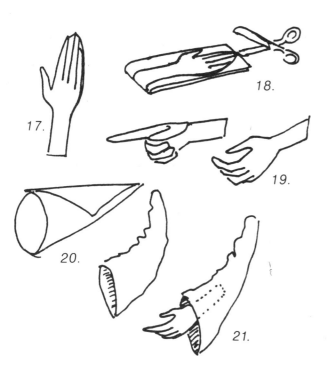

Sleeves These are made from more cones. This time they are squashed and wrinkled into the shape you want.

You can close up her bottom by gluing her down to another flat piece.

When the glue has set, tear away the surplus and she's ready for painting, or any other decorative touches you care to add.

If You Want Her to Fly She'll Need Legs

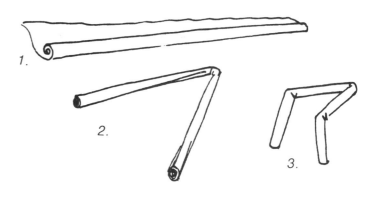

Both legs can be made from one tube. It's a good idea to make this tube by rolling your paper around a piece of wire or a knitting needle or a thin dowel.

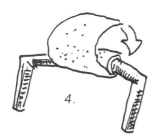

4.

Her pants (4) are a strip of white or pink (or black) paper wrapped around the leg tube at the proper location.

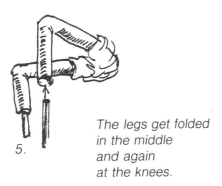

5.

The legs get folded in the middle and again at the knees.

Shoes Roll up two small tubes that will slip into the ends of the legs. These will become her heels as well as the thing that connects her feet to her legs. The final shape of the shoe comes from wrapping with glued strips of torn paper bag. Use small thin strips and don't be afraid to experiment.

The shoe starts with another tube that wraps around the heel and becomes the base for the shoe.

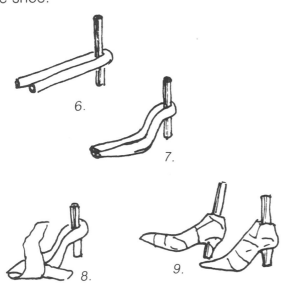

6.

7.

8.

9.

The completed legs get glued to her bottom (10).

10.

BUILDING A FIRE UNDER THE OLD POT

A small lightbulb under the cauldron can make it look like something is really cooking.

Firewood, made from little sticks or rolled up paper, and flames of red, yellow, and orange tissue paper can make the scene even more real.

The Witch's Cauldron

Wrap a ball with aluminum foil or wax paper. Then cover half of it with strips.

Use dry grocery bag strips with torn edges. Glue every place where one strip crosses another. Finish with small pieces brushed with glue.

On a piece of stiff stock draw a circle about twice as big as the ball.

Draw a second line on the inside to make a rim. Now you just — cut that out!

Wind the rim to the best shape and glue.

Take out the ball before you glue the rim to the cauldron.

Cover the whole thing with small glued pieces.

Legs: Are three small cones like noses.

BROOMS

You can make broomsticks from any round stick. Sucker sticks are just great and small dowels work very well.

Some great sticks are barbecue skewers — you can find them in shops that sell things from the Orient. They come in packs of 100 and they are quite inexpensive.

Puppet Witches

A rolled up paper tube, with its top split into many strips, can be glued inside for a control that works from underneath.

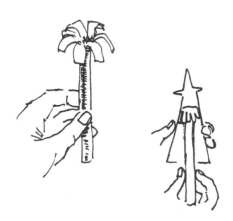

Flying Witches

A good way to suspend your witch is to tie a loop around a small strip of paper and glue it to the tip of her hat.

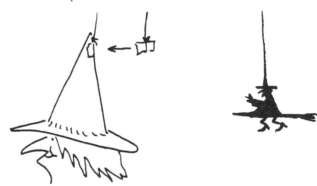

To operate from above, thread your string through her hat and tie the ends to a control stick.

BAT MOBILE

You can build a great mobile from one old gnarled tree branch with a bunch of bats suspended on thread or fishline.

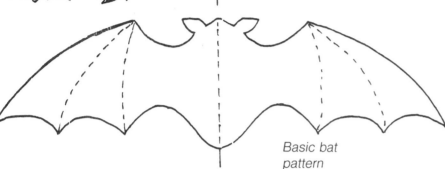

Basic bat pattern

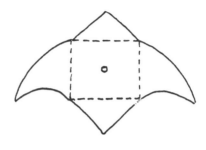

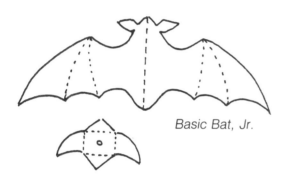

Basic Bat, Jr.

For balance — tie a bit of paper to your thread for an anchor and pass the thread up through the hole.

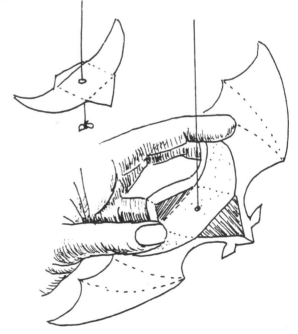

These bats are made of two pieces. The small, bird-shaped piece that gets glued to the back of the wings helps the bat keep its shape and provides a place to attach the support thread.

Each bat needs a weight — like a pin or nail — glued to the center fold.

The pin or nail glued to the inside of the center line gives the bat a lower center of gravity for better balance.

The Final Balancing Act

To get your bats to pose just the way you want them, you will need to add bits of paper, as weights, to the wings.

It takes a bit of patience.

CARS

from Cardboard

Once you get the hang of basic car building, you can just let your imagination take over. Trucks, tanks, dozers, vans, campers, classics, hot rods, stockers, formula racers, or the vehicle of your dreams.

You might also have fun building roads, raceways, and service stations.

Basic Cars

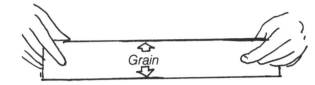

Grain

Matching the end will tell you if your strip is parallel.

Start with a strip of cardboard that has been carefully cut with straight-parallel edges and the grain running the short way.

Overlap the ends and glue them together to make a ring.

With the glue joint on the bottom, shape the ring into a profile (outline shape) of your car.

Put a fairly generous line of glue along one edge of the profile and glue it down to another sheet of cardboard.

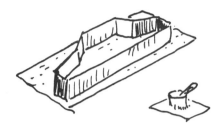

When the glue is quite dry, trim carefully around the profile.

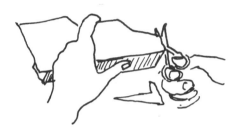

Fingernail Scissors Work Best for Trimming around Profiles.

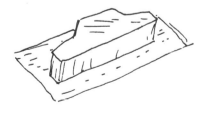

After you've trimmed the first size, put glue on the other edge and stick it on another sheet of cardboard.

When the glue is dry, trim it and smooth it.

If you find places where the glue has pulled away — take your applicator and force more glue into the crack. If you have a gap, pull the edges together with masking tape. Once the edge is secured, take off the tape.

Use sandpaper to smooth up the edges. And it's a good idea to give your car an overall prime coat of thin glue.

Nail Polish

Don't overlook this important discovery. Nail polish is a lacquer just like they use on expensive custom cars. It comes in wild, fantastic colors and looks great on little cars.

Customize those cars with details made of wads and bits of paper. Copy your favorite or design a dream car. Then spackle, smooth, and paint.

WHEELS

Four strips of paper or cardboard the same length and width will give you good basic wheels — if you have black paper, it's great for tires. White strips on the inside with black on the outside will give you a good set of whitewalls.

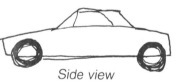

Wind tires on a pencil or a dowel.

Wheels can be just glued to the body.

Side view   *Rear view*

Strips of cardboard can be fitted over the wheels and trimmed to the shape you like.

Headlights and taillights can be colored paper or paint — chrome details can be made from scraps of foil wrap.

If you build a separate chassis, with front and rear suspension units, you can cut away the wheel wells and mount the wheels inside the line of the body.

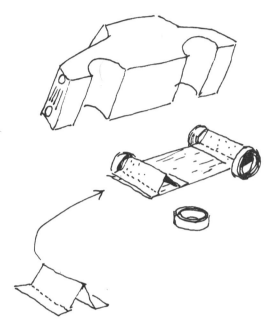

Fold up ridge for suspension unit and glue to chassis panel.

Snap fasteners make fine wheels. Try a fabric store or a dime store. Even supermarkets have snaps sometimes.

Fit them inside the tires.

You can paint and decorate these cars with anything — but a final finish with several coats of spray paint can make them really shine.

MORE COMPLEX WHEELS

It's tough to make round things, and small round things are the toughest.

Paper Punch One good answer for very small things is the paper punch. Most punches make a ¼ inch disc, but larger or smaller punches can be found by searching.

Punch Dies Your hardware store can get you punch dies that come in many sizes. They are sharp on one end, and you place them on your cardboard on top of an end grain wood block and bang them with a hammer. Every whack gives you another round disc.

It's a good idea to wear safety glasses when using punch dies.

Washer Wheels The hardware store also has lots of different types and sizes of washers — you may find just what you need.

Nail, Washer, Bead Combinations Roll up a tight paper tube for an axle — slip the washer onto a nail followed by a bead to make a smooth surface — then slip the nail into the tube and adjust it so the wheel turns freely, and glue.

Bead and Strip Wheels A strip of cardboard wrapped around a bead makes a workable wheel. The bead is a bearing, so the wheel will turn smoothly.

Here's a Tool for Finding the Centers in Wheels

Make sure the two angle strips are exactly the same distance from the center line.

Place any size wheel disc in the "V" and snug it up against both strips. Lay a straightedge against the two nails on the center line and draw a line on the disc. Rotate the disc and draw another line. Where the two cross is the center of the disc.

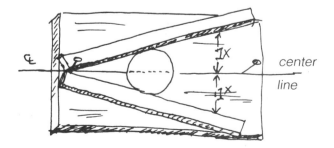

Mini Cars

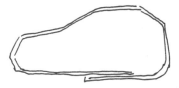

These cars are quick and easy to build and lots of fun to play with.

Down at the bottom of the page are the sizes for the cardboard strips you need. Start with a basic shape and glue it to another piece of cardboard that just comes up to the edge of the windows.

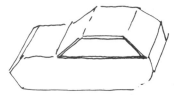

When that is dry, trim the edges and do the other side.

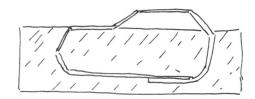

Use a pencil to roll up the wheels and then glue them onto the body.

Customizing Touches

Add-on panels for styling

Draw your own license tags.

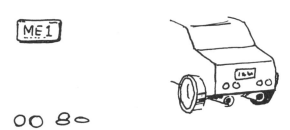

Punch out taillights from bright red paper.

Paper or foil tubes make exhaust stacks.

Body Strip	(Make sure about your grain)	⇧ Grain ⇩

1	Wheel	3	Strips
2		4	

Cut from lightweight cardboard.

A Few Basic Body Shapes

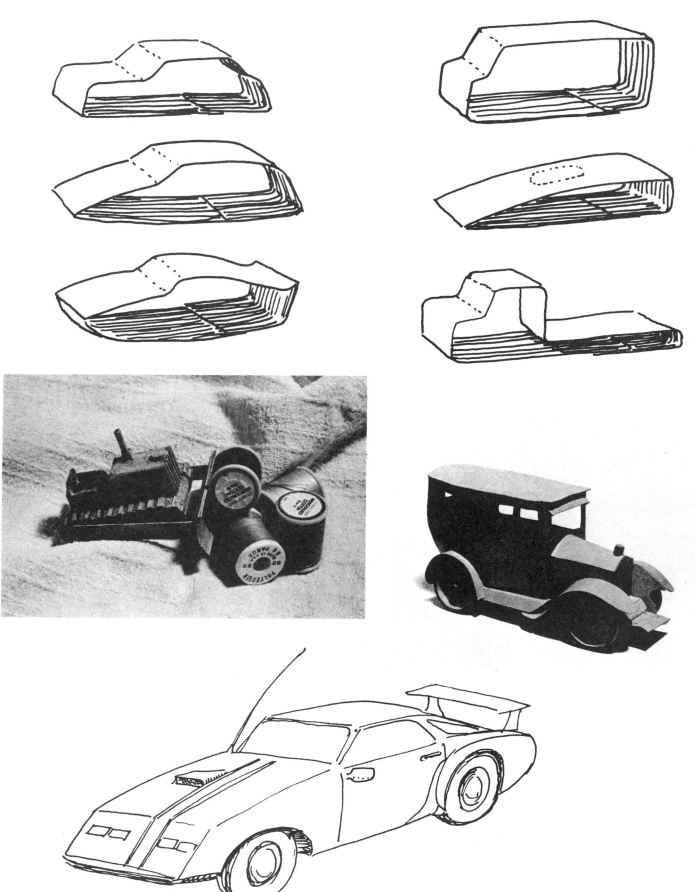

FUN TRUCKIN'

Start with the cab, 1. Then add your truck bed.

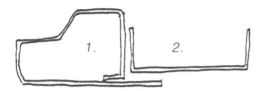

When you glue the side on this pickup, it covers both the cab and the bed.

Once you get started, there are lots of trucks to think about.

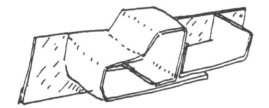

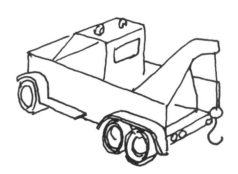

Bigger trucks get more wheels.

THE BEAM COMPASS

A Cheap Simple Tool to Help You Make Big Circles

1. A wood or metal beam
2. A sharp metal point that marks the center of your circle
3. A movable marker that can be slid along the beam and locked in place at any point

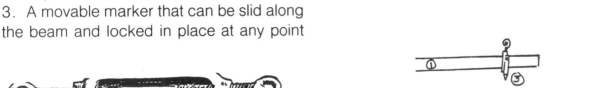

A common turnbuckle, available from the hardware or builders' supply store (This becomes the adjustable marker.)

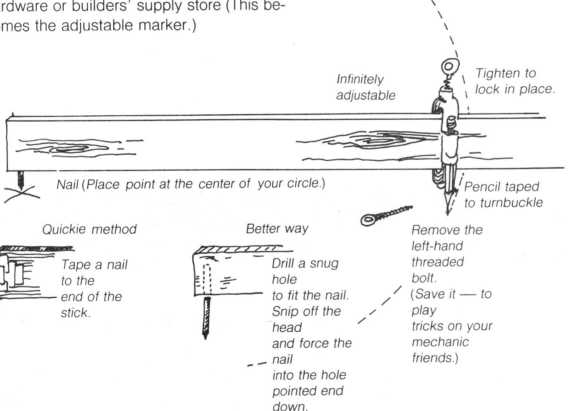

Infinitely adjustable

Tighten to lock in place.

Nail (*Place point at the center of your circle.*)

Pencil taped to turnbuckle

Quickie method

Tape a nail to the end of the stick.

Better way

Drill a snug hole to fit the nail. Snip off the head and force the nail into the hole pointed end down.

Remove the left-hand threaded bolt. (*Save it — to play tricks on your mechanic friends.*)

Notes

You can generally find the wood you need in the same place that has the turnbuckles. Choose a straight, smooth dry piece and try your turnbuckle on it to make sure it fits.

Hardwood is nicer than soft, but it's not critical.

If you really want to go first class, use a standard-size aluminum strip.

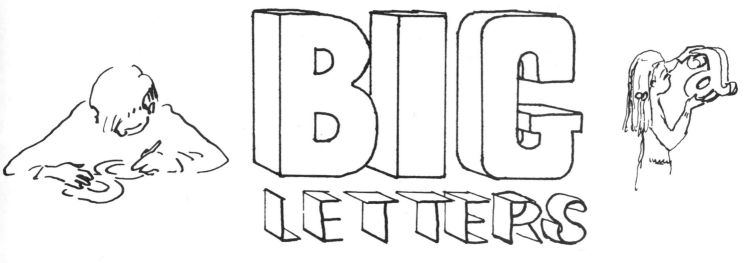

BIG LETTERS

IT'S A NEAT WAY TO GET AN "A"

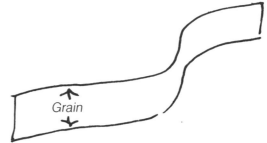

Grain

Cut cardboard strips long enough to outline your letter (make sure the grain is going the short way). The width of your strips will set the thickness of the finished letter.

Draw the letter or letters you like — carefully — on a piece of cardboard and cut them out as neatly as you can.

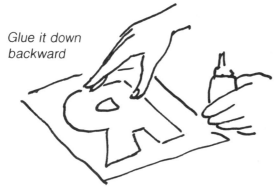

Glue it down backward

Glue your letter down, *backward,* to another piece of cardboard.

Run a line of glue around the edge of the letter and then carefully glue the strip in place. This takes a bit of patience, but it's worth it.

Reinforcing Corner Seams

When you have the front the way you want it, run a line of glue along the back edge and stick your letter down on another sheet of cardboard.

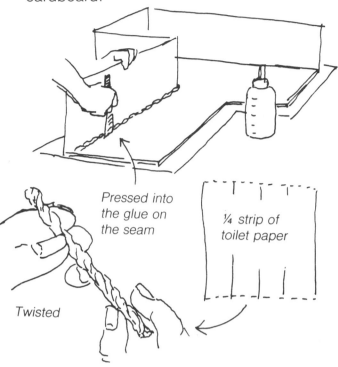

Pressed into the glue on the seam

¼ strip of toilet paper

Twisted

When the glue has set — trim your letter and smooth the edges with sandpaper.

Finally — trim the back edge and paint.

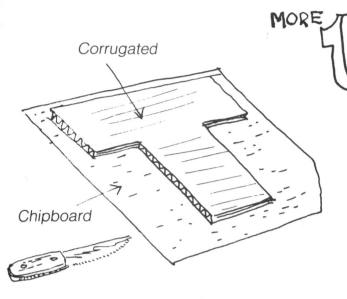

Corrugated

Chipboard

Glue line

If you are willing to put out a bit more energy, you will find that corrugated cardboard that comes from old cartons works even better for the inside profile pieces. Cut them out with an ordinary serrated-edged kitchen knife and glue them down to your chipboard or what ever cardboard you choose for the outsides.

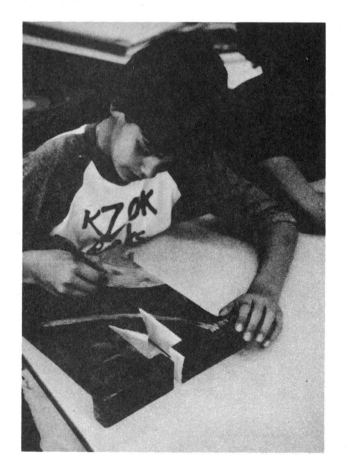

The thickness of the corrugated will give you a better edge for gluing and the corrugated affords better strength and helps to keep the surfaces smoother.

A serrated-edged kitchen knife works fine for corrugated — but don't try to slice it — use the knife like a little saw.

When your side strips are dry, trim the edges as neatly as you can and then sand off any lumpy places.

If you want a slick smooth finish, cover the surfaces with a thin coat of vinyl paste spackle. Sand the spackle and you will have a smooth clean surface for your finishing.

I find that ordinary latex house paint is a good cheap undercoat. I look for it at garage sales and secondhand outlets. Any light color will do, as it's only a sealer coat. I put the color on later.

If you aren't a very neat worker . . . don't give up. Just stick your thing together with a general sort of roughness and don't try to fake it. You might even like to paste other bits and pieces on the surface or make it into a collage.

Those Darn Paper Cups

Sometimes you just have to use paper or plastic cups for paints. There is a way to fix them so they work quite well.

The problem with the cups is they are too tall and they have narrow bottoms. So! Chop them off at half-mast, turn the tops over, and slip the bottoms inside.

Now you've got a short cup with a wide bottom.

BUILDING BUILDINGS

Making Your Own Boxes
and Rectangles

To really understand things we sometimes have to take them apart. Then we find the basic shapes that fit together to make up the whole structure.

Lots of buildings are made up of squares and rectangles and triangles. Together, these forms can make some exciting combinations.

These box shapes are easy to make from cardboard strips of different lengths and widths.

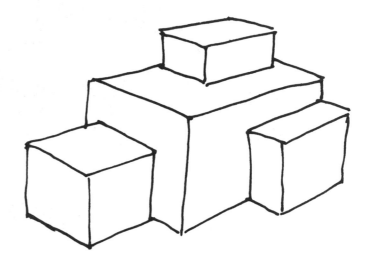

1. Make a short fold at one end of the strip, for gluing. Bring the other end around it and glue it.

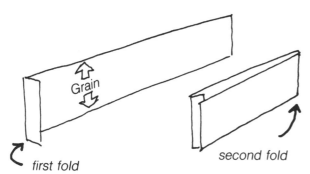

first fold

second fold

2. To make square boxes just fold once more to bring the ends together and you have four sides.

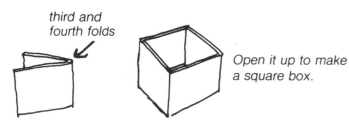

third and fourth folds

Open it up to make a square box.

3. Rectangles start like the squares, but you make the third fold in just one side so it gives you a long and a short part. Squeeze the third fold flat and press out the rest of the strip to find fold number 4.

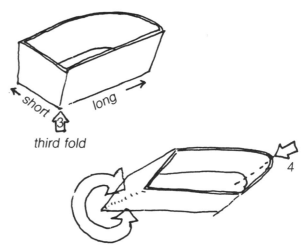

short   *long*

third fold

4. Squeeze the third fold flat and the fourth fold will come up at the far end.

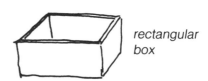

rectangular box

A Plan for a Small Building

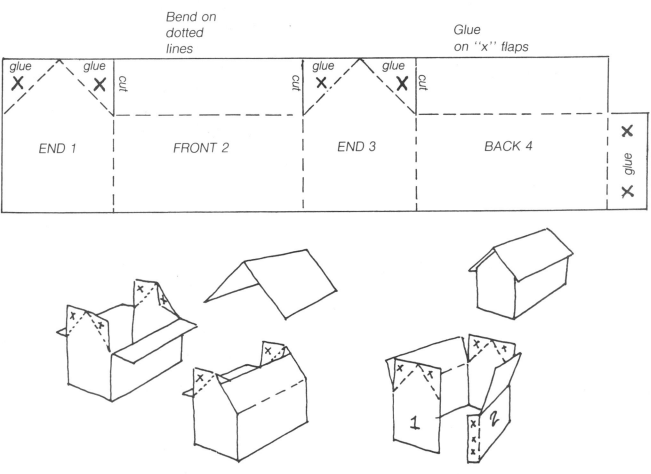

Windows, Doors, and Other Details

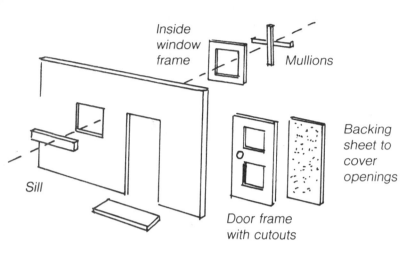

Inside window frame

Mullions

Sill

Door frame with cutouts

Backing sheet to cover openings

Barns often have "gambrel roofs." Some barns have thin vertical strips about every foot.

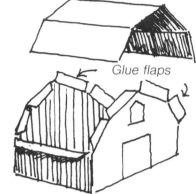

Glue flaps

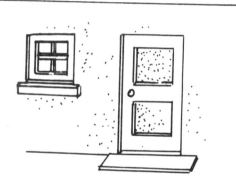

The window and door frames glue on the inside. Mullions and door go inside the frames — sills go outside.

This silo roof is made from two cones.

Two cones

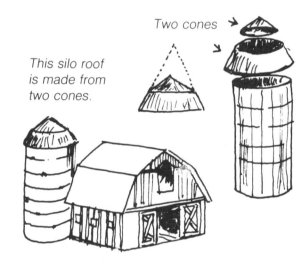

Board siding (called "clapboards") can be made with cardboard strips — start at the bottom and let each board overlap the board below it.

Shingles can be made from strips cut halfway through and put on like board siding.

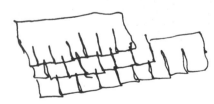

Exposed timbers can be cut from colored paper or cardboard.

PAPER LOGS

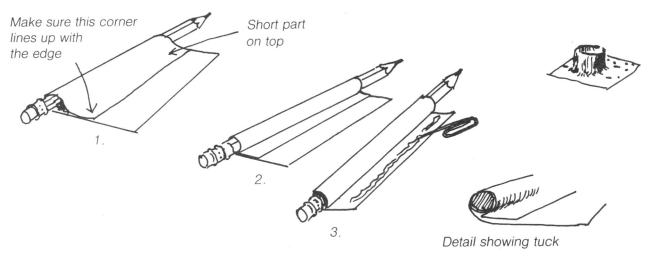

Make sure this corner lines up with the edge

Short part on top

1.

2.

3.

Detail showing tuck

1. Use rectangles of any kind of paper — be sure they are all the same size if you want the logs to be the same.
Bring the short end of the paper over the pencil and make sure the corner lines up with the edge of the bottom piece.
2. Press the paper tight against the pencil, and with the ends of your fingers tuck the top paper under the pencil as you begin to roll up your log.

3. Keep the roll tight, and when you are near the end put a line of glue along the edge.
4. Wind up the log — smooth out any lumps — slip out the pencil, and go on to the next.

Building with Logs

The trick with these logs is to alternate them at the corners so you don't need notches to make them fit together.

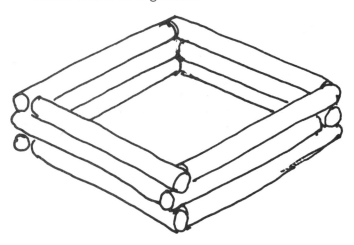

A line of glue along the top of each layer of logs sticks them all together.

Note: You may find it easier to plan out the walls and build each one separately so they can lie flat until the glue is dry.

Window sash can be cut out of cardboard. Make the outside framework so it fits inside the opening, then cut out the inside and add the thin strips (called mullions).

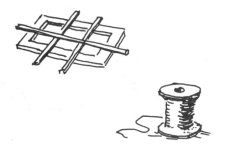

You can make mullions from thin strips, broom straws, wire, spaghetti, toothpicks, noodles or? Glue them on the inside and trim off the ends.

A very realistic door can be made by gluing grocery bag paper strips onto a cardboard door.

They look just like boards, and with a pen you can put in the nailheads.

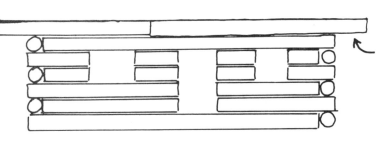

Frames for the doors and windows are made from cardboard boards fitted to the openings.

This longer log sticks out on the ends to hold up the roof — you may need to make it in two pieces.

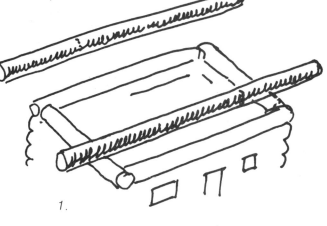

1. Long logs go on each side of the cabin. They stick out a way past the ends.

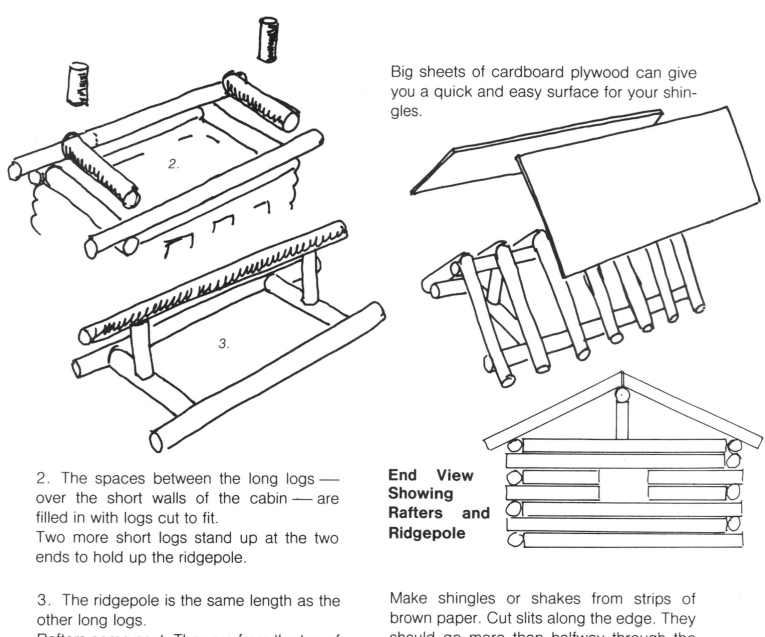

Big sheets of cardboard plywood can give you a quick and easy surface for your shingles.

2. The spaces between the long logs — over the short walls of the cabin — are filled in with logs cut to fit.
Two more short logs stand up at the two ends to hold up the ridgepole.

3. The ridgepole is the same length as the other long logs.
Rafters come next. They run from the top of the ridge down past the walls to make an overhanging edge.

End View Showing Rafters and Ridgepole

Make shingles or shakes from strips of brown paper. Cut slits along the edge. They should go more than halfway through the strip. Put your shingles on from the bottom edge and work up to the ridge. Lay one strip over the strip below, just like real shingles.

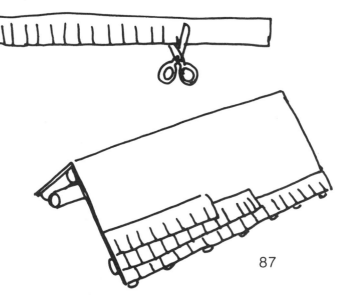

PAPER TIMBERS

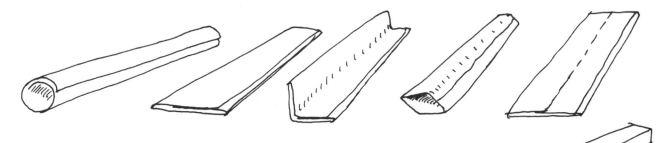

Paper timbers start with tubes, rolled on a pencil or a dowel. Try not to make them more than two layers thick. Flatten the tube to give you two edges, then fold it over to make two more.

Open it up and flatten it again so the second set of edges are firmly set.

Then open it up with a pencil to make a nice square timber.

Here are a few examples of how you can put your timbers together — just cut the ends, fold out the flaps, and glue. ("X" indicates some places to glue.)

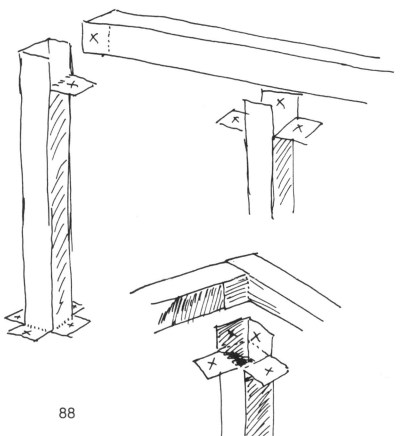

Try some high-rise towers. You will be amazed at how high you can go.

The TREE HOUSE

Building tree stumps is easy. Start with a
framework of cardboard strips, then cover it
with wrinkly chunks of glued paper to create
the rough textures of a gnarled old stump.

Cardboard Grain

You need lots of cardboard strips for this
project. Tin snips are good tools for cutting
cardboard.

Stick one or more strips together to make a
ring the size you want for the top of your
stump.

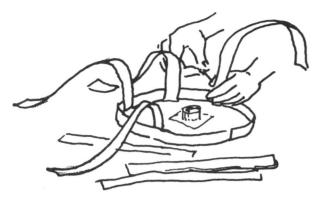

As your stump takes shape you can add on limbs, roots, and other special touches.

Keep in mind the openings you want —you may want both a front and a back door.

Attach six to a dozen strips to the ring, and when they are dry, turn the whole thing over and glue the other ends to a big cardboard or wood base. This will give you the general shape and a frame to build on. Stick those ends down with glue and hold them, till they dry, with masking tape — THEN REMOVE THAT TAPE.

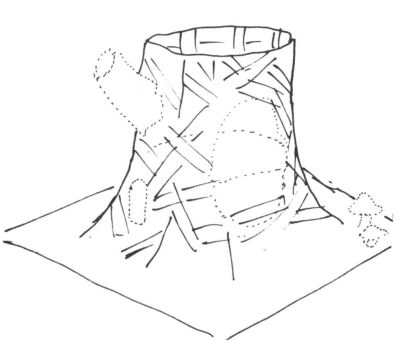

A large opening is needed if you plan to play in the tree house.

Build up your stump with lots of strips — be sure to glue each place where one strip passes over another.

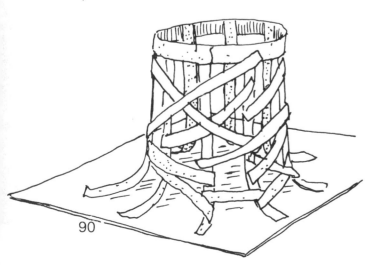

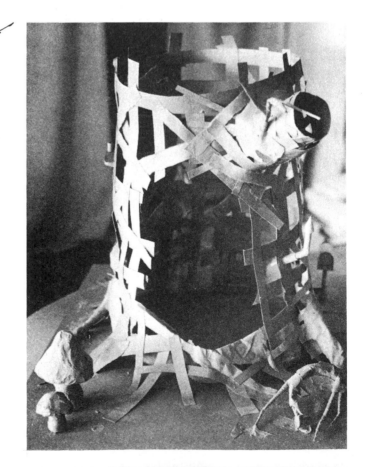

Twisty Roots and Branches

Build roots on twisted paper cores. Bend, taper and shape them into a natural form and finish them off with wrinkled paper bark. Use bark to hide any un-treelike parts.

Thumb Mushrooms Use very thin strips — start with a ring around your thumb, then a loop over the end of the thumb. Complete the form with more glued strips.

Make the stem from a tube. Tear or cut the ends so they can bend out to glue inside the cap and onto the ground.

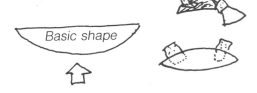

Fungus Cut a number of different sizes and bend them into a curved shape. Put paper hinges on the back edge to glue the fungus to the tree.

Basic shape

Bark You can hardly miss when you cover old tree trunks. Wrinkly chunks of glued paper, with torn edges, make it easy to create rough textures that seem natural. See "Paper Skins," page 10 for instructions.

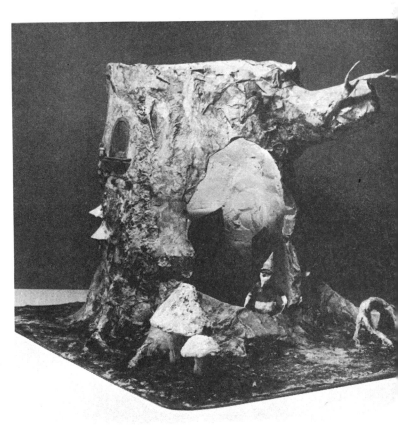

The addition of a few rocks, twigs, and dried leaves can give your stump a very natural look.

This sheltered door adds a cozy touch. It is made from two cardboard pieces and glued on with grocery bag strips.

There is just no end to the funny imaginative things you can think up to add to a fantasy project like this.

REMEMBER
Masking tape is great stuff, but temporary. Don't leave it inside your projects.

92

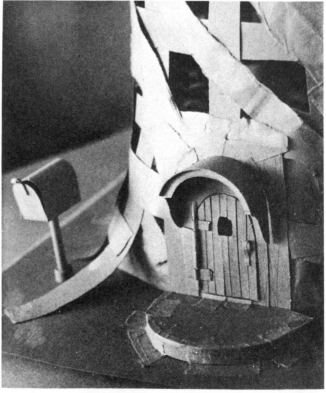

Door Details

 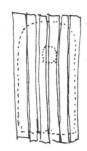 

Cardboard door & frame *Cardboard boards glued to door* *Trimmed door*

Hinges

Paper hinges

Note how they are shaped to fit the toothpick.

Glue to frame *Glue to door*

Round toothpick

Watch how you position your hinges —your door has to hang from them.

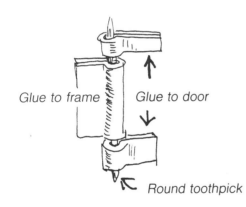

Pattern for door handle

door handle shape

Or try your own design.

Other Funky Stuff

Flowerpots

 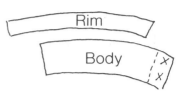

Rim

Body

Shape the body then add the rim at the top.

Window Boxes are just little boxes that go under your windows.

A Boot Scraper can be made from an ''H''-shaped piece of cardboard with the longer bottom legs folded for support.

Windows can be made from bits of clear plastic.

Shutters are like the door, made to fit the window and split down the center.

and . . . Don't forget the door mat.

WELCOME

FUNKY CHIMNEYS

Start with the old "paper-rolled-around-a-pencil" trick and then make a smaller roll that will fit inside. (But don't glue them together just yet.)

Cut the big tube in two, on an angle so the pieces can be glued back together with a bend. Put glue on the small tube and slide it inside the joint to add strength.

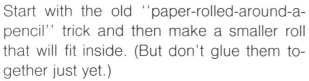

Cut on an angle

Inner roll   Outer roll

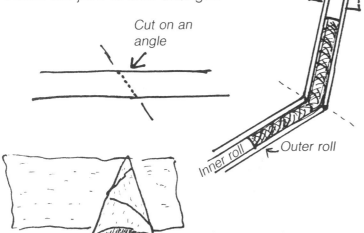

A grocery bag strip can be twisted into a cone to make the rain cap. Make it big and trim it to size.

Connect the chimney with a "flashing" made from a square of paper with a cardboard ring just big enough to fit snugly around the pipe.

R.F.D.* MAILBOX

Draw the patterns for parts 1 and 2 onto some cardboard. (Watch the grain.) Cut them out and fold part 2 on the dotted lines.

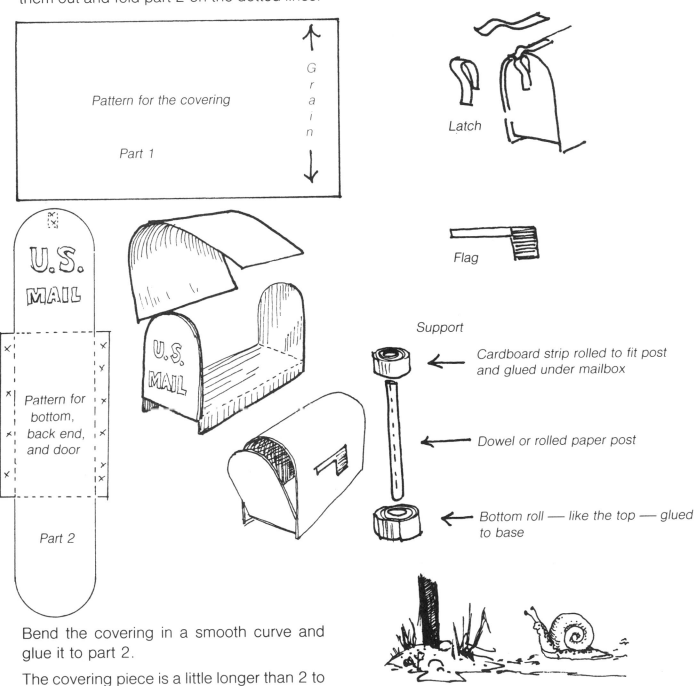

Pattern for the covering

Part 1

G
r
a
i
n

U.S. MAIL

Pattern for bottom, back end, and door

Part 2

Latch

Flag

Support

Cardboard strip rolled to fit post and glued under mailbox

Dowel or rolled paper post

Bottom roll — like the top — glued to base

Bend the covering in a smooth curve and glue it to part 2.

The covering piece is a little longer than 2 to make a projected edge in the back and a place for the door to fit into in front.

* Rural Free Delivery

The base of the post can be hidden under some paper lumps plus grass and rocks and stuff.

CASTLES

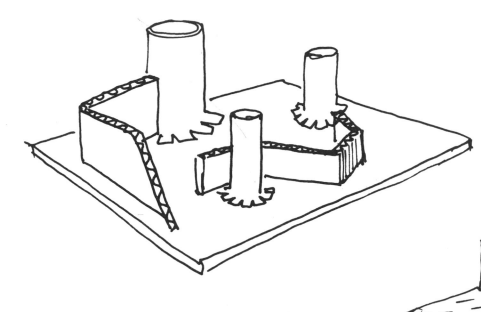

Starting Your Castle

Start with a base of cardboard or wood, some plain towers with their bottoms flared out and glued down solid give you a very good start, and a few strips cut from a corrugated carton can be the base for your landscaping.

Use some pieces of cardboard to make the large flat areas.

The cliffs are made with crumpled-up grocery bag paper — you don't need to wet it — just glue the edges.

You will be surprised at how easy it is to build very realistic terrain.

Real rocks, sticks, dried weeds add interesting touches and, in the end, paint will make it both colorful and strong.

SQUARE TOWERS

The main part of the tower is made with a strip that has the four walls plus a short piece that will be the glue flap.

The dashed lines show where to fold the walls; the glue flap will go inside. You may want to cut out the windows before you glue the walls together.

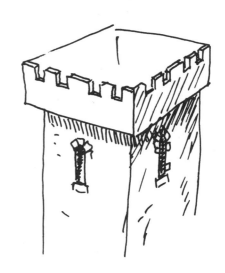

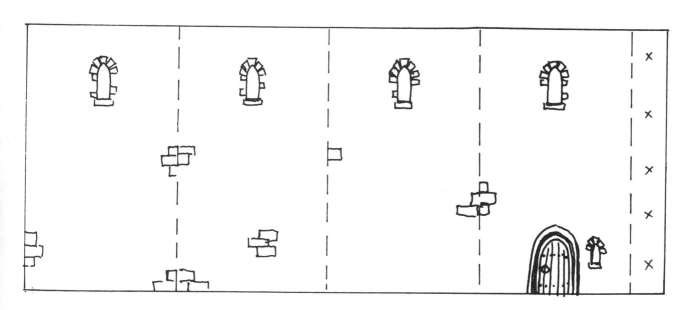

Pattern for a Square Tower

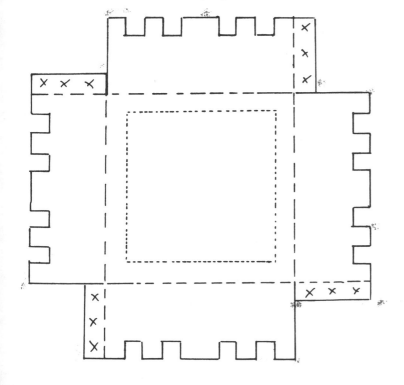

At the top of the tower you need battlements. They stick out over the walls to make it difficult for enemies to get inside.

In the plan I've drawn, the floor and the walls are all one piece — transfer the pattern to some cardboard, then cut-score-fold and glue. The dotted lines show how it fits on the tower.

ROUND TOWERS

Start by making a tube the size you want your tower. Use sturdy paper or lightweight cardboard.

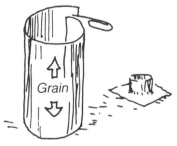

Take special care to be sure about the grain and you will find it easy to build tower tubes of any size and you will never have to look for discarded towel rolls again.

You may want to cut any openings in the towers before you glue.

The roof is made with circles about twice as big as your tower. You can use a compass and measure accurately or just find something round that's about the right size and trace it onto paper or light cardboard.

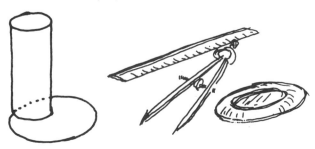

The roof circles become cones when you cut one of the lines and wind them up and glue them.

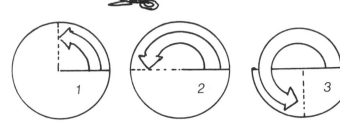

The first cone overlaps just one quarter, the second, two quarters, and the third can be made with a half-circle wound upon itself.

Cut short slits along the bottoms of the smaller cones.

Put glue on the flaps of #2 cone and press it down on cone #1, then do the same to add #3 to the top of the stack.

Cut short slits around the top of your tower. Bend the flaps *out* and put glue on them.

Then press the roof down firmly so the flaps bend up inside the edge of the roof.

If any flaps stick out — wait till they are dry and trim off the offending parts.

WALLS

Here is a short wall that might run between two towers. The folded-out part, at the top, lets the people inside drop nasty things on unwanted visitors.

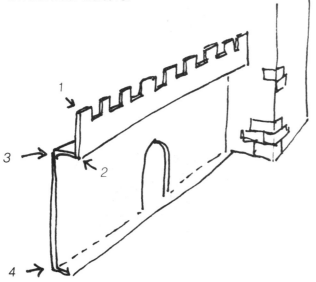

The holes along the top are for shooting and ducking.

When walls fit against round towers you have to cut the walkways so they fit the curve.

Layout for a short wall showing folding lines. Make your own wall to fit the size of your castle.

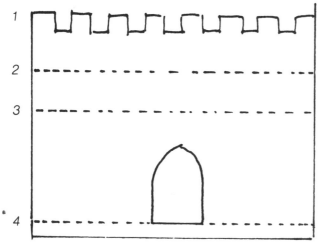

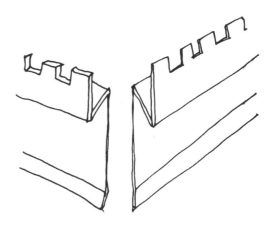

When you have a corner with no tower you can cut the walkways at an angle — like the corner of a picture frame — and join the parts with paper patches.

The gate is guarded by two six-sided towers. The gate is in a wall between the towers. A drawbridge, leading across the moat, can be pulled up from inside the towers.

Towers

Make the towers first, from lightweight cardboard. Make them to a scale that will fit your castle.

Take your time laying out the towers — the more accurate they are, the easier it will be to fit them together.

Score and fold along the lines and cut out the openings. I suggest an X-acto knife or a pair of toenail scissors.

Glue a strip of GBP* along one edge. Then bring the other edge up to make a nice, flush joint. The strip — on the inside — makes it easy to do a strong, neat job of joining.

* Grocery Bag Paper

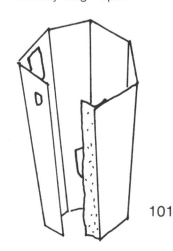

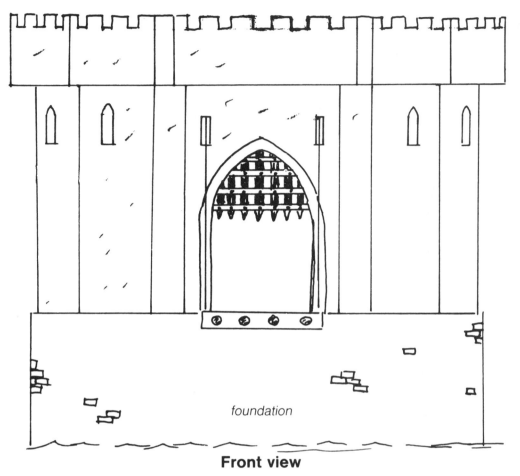

Front view

looking across the moat

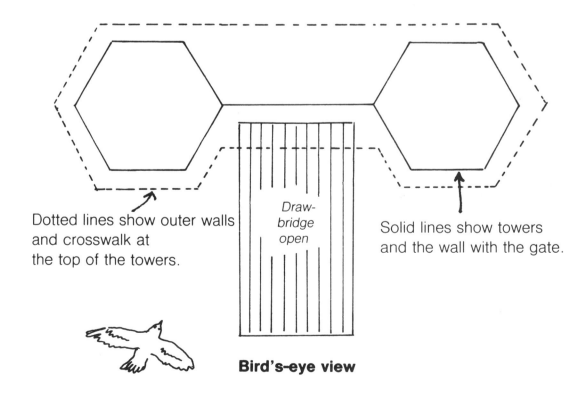

Dotted lines show outer walls
and crosswalk at
the top of the towers.

*Draw-
bridge
open*

Solid lines show towers
and the wall with the gate.

Bird's-eye view

The Gate

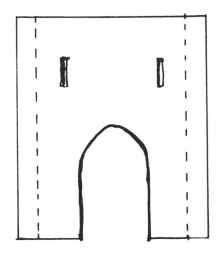

Pattern for the gate wall with openings for the drawbridge cables.

Use the base to get the gate and the two towers all lined up.

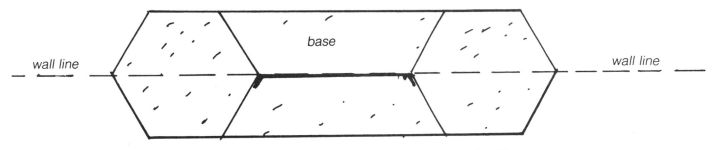

wall line

base

wall line

Cardboard base with location for towers and gate drawn in

You can put the parts together with upper hinges soaked in glue. Wrap them over and around the edges for extra support.

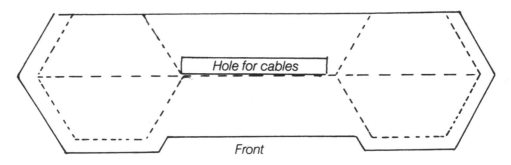

Hole for cables

Front

This is a layout for the upper part of the towers. The dotted lines show where the towers fit together and the solid lines show the overhang.

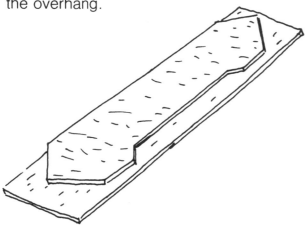

Cut out a cardboard profile and glue it to a larger piece of cardboard.

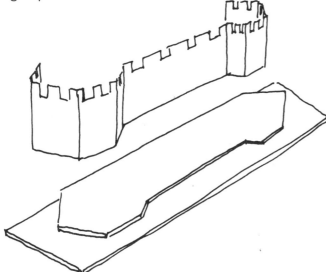

Cut a long strip for the walls (make sure the grain is running the short way). Then fit it to your profile. Make a good, sharp fold at each corner.

Take your time and be sure you have a good fit — then glue it down and trim the bottom edge.

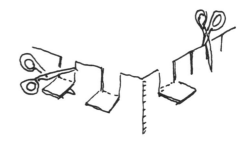

There is an easy way to make those holes in the top of the wall. Just make a series of cuts down from the edge. Fold over the parts that you want to take out and cut them off — flush to the wall. Now the top of your wall is *crenelated.*

Finally, glue the upper part to the top of the towers.

Exploded view of castle— all the pieces

The Drawbridge

The bridge is just a cardboard rectangle with short sides that fold up to add strength and rigidity.

The drawbridge has a hinge at one end and a counterweight at the other. The hinge can be made with paper strips looped over a dowel or a wire.

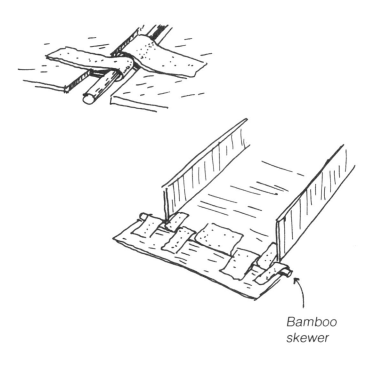

Bamboo skewer

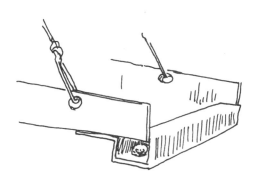

The bamboo skewers from the Chinese grocery are just great.

This part of the hinge glues down in front of the gate — be sure you leave room in front of the door for the sides when the gate goes up.

The counterweight is needed to pull the bridge down when you unwind the cables.

Build a box that will fit across under the end of the bridge. A few clean stones will do for weights — close up the open ends with glue-coated paper patches.

The Windlass

The windlass is made from a dowel or a strong paper tube that has been shaped by winding on a dowel.

It fits into a simple cardboard box support that has slots at the narrow ends to fit the shaft.

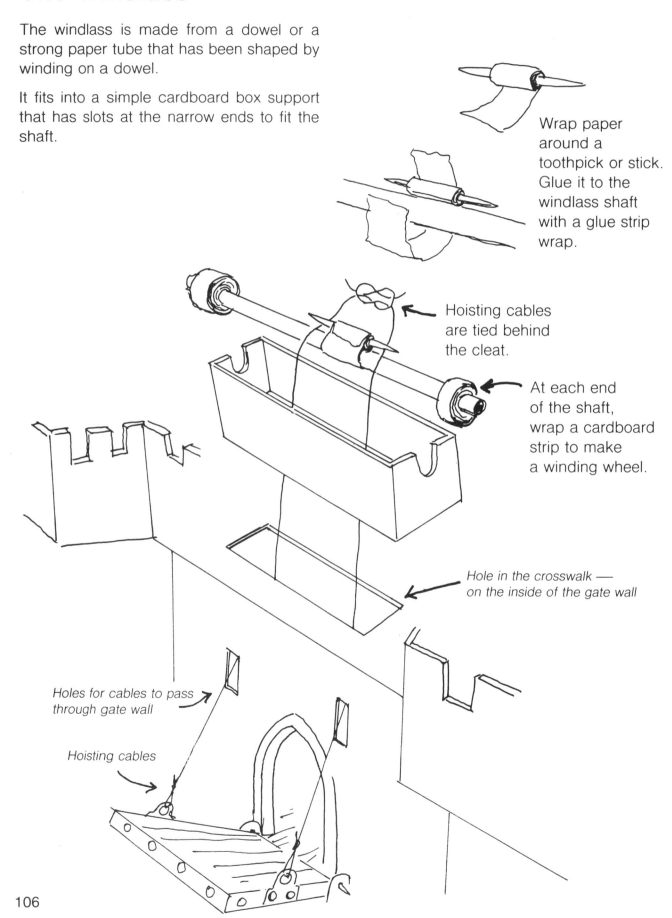

Wrap paper around a toothpick or stick. Glue it to the windlass shaft with a glue strip wrap.

Hoisting cables are tied behind the cleat.

At each end of the shaft, wrap a cardboard strip to make a winding wheel.

Hole in the crosswalk — on the inside of the gate wall

Holes for cables to pass through gate wall

Hoisting cables

Decorating Your Castle

Two or three layers of cardboard trim around the doors give a real look of stonework.

Add wood grain and nail marks to timbers and planks with a fine pen. Then color them with watercolors.

A plain window

The same window with decorative stonework drawn around it

Fluttering pennants can be made from bits snipped from old magazines. Fold double, cut out the shape, then glue it around a sewing pin.

Vines often climb up castle walls, and don't forget that spiders, frogs, lizards, bugs, and little mice are often found in cracks and hidden corners.

You don't have to draw every brick or stone to get the effect — just a few here and there will do the trick.

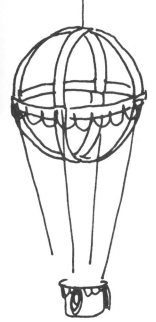

X AND O CONSTRUCTION

This is a way to build large, round shapes, by making big cardboard X's and O's. Spheres and hemispheres are basic structures that can set your imagination free. If you cover them with paper skins, and build up details with wads and other stuff, you will be able to make any- thing — well, almost anything.

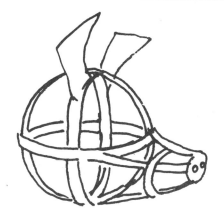

Think of them as forms you can build on.

Basic X's and O's

Grain (1)

1. Start with three strips of cardboard. Make sure the grain is running the short way.

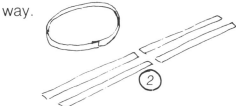

2. Make a ring from one of the strips and cut the other two in half.

3. Use the four short strips to make two crosses. Curve the arms of the crosses.

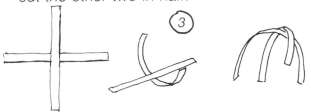

4. And glue one into the ring.

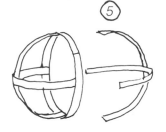

5. Glue the legs of the other cross to the ring, right over the ends of the first legs.

6. Now you have a *sphere,* and you have converted some two-dimensional strips into a 3-D solid.

As you build up your structure — by adding more cardboard strips — try to put glue on every point where one strip crosses over another strip.

The Three-Ring

Alternative

This method also starts with three strips (with the grain running the short way).

Make the strips into three rings.

Slip one ring inside another and glue them at the north and south poles.

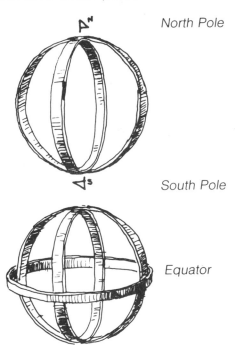

North Pole

South Pole

Equator

Finally, slip the third ring over the other two, place it at the equator, and glue at all four contact points.

RHINOS

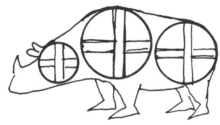

Ears and horn are small cones.

The rhino is highest at the shoulders and has a small head that sort of fits into his big muscular neck.

The head and neck are shaped a lot like the end of your thumb. Can you imagine the horn coming out of your thumbnail and the ears sticking out of your first knuckle? Then the shoulders would be back at your second knuckle. Shake hands with a rhino.

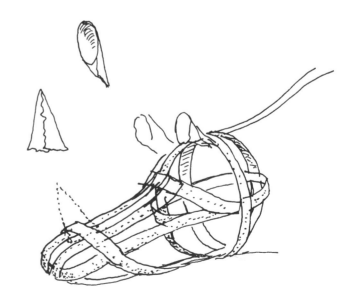

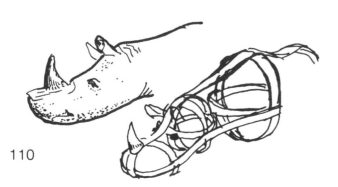

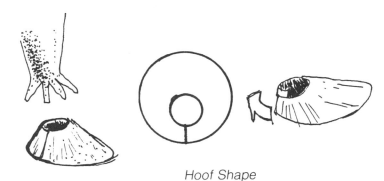

The legs, horn, and ears are glued to the body framework with the torn flaps. The bottom ends of the legs are cut or torn to fit the hooves.

To make the legs all about the same size, start by making a triangular pattern. Wrap grocery bag paper around the pattern to make a cone. Remove the pattern and glue the edge (make four).

Hoof Shape

Shape the cone and then tear or cut the big end to make a lot of flaps to glue the legs onto the body.

The hooves are made from cardboard circles with smaller circles on one side. Form them into slanted cones with the hole at the back.

Fill in the framework of the head and body with more thin strips.

HAPPY HIPPOS

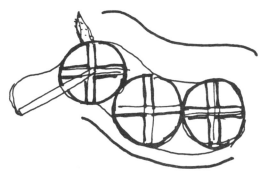

Three spheres make the head and torso of this hippo. Join them with strips.

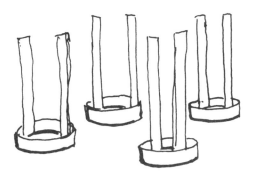

The feet are rings with strips reaching up to make legs.

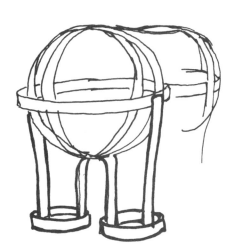

Front and back legs go on the front and back spheres.

Use more strips to fill out the body and then add front and back strips to each foot to round out the legs.

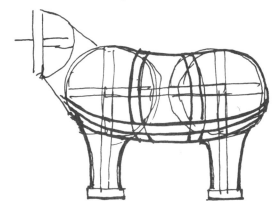

Make the ears from paper cones. The jaw is shaped like the bottom of a guitar.

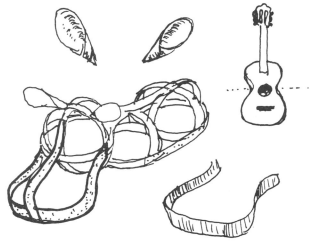

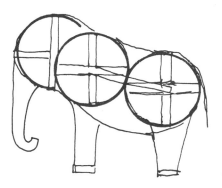

The elephant has a sloping body — the front sphere is higher than the rear. The head's not a full sphere and it's mounted a bit higher than the shoulder — it will help if you keep your spheres lined up horizontally and vertically.

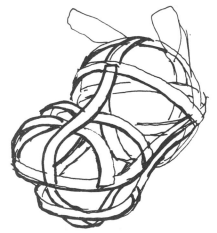

Use thin strips to build up the head and the lower jaw. This is a good example of cage-type construction.

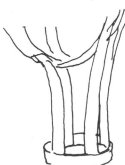

Legs start with rings for feet and 4 strips that attach to the body spheres.

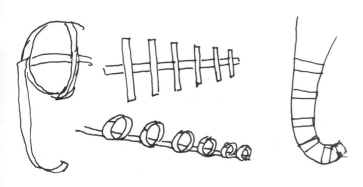

The mouth is made with two short strips glued together to make an "L" and the ends glued to the head under the trunk.

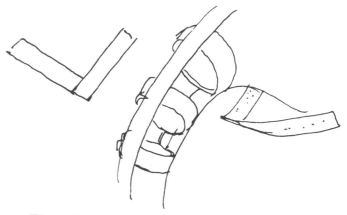

Start the trunk with a strip shaped like the front outline of the trunk.

Lay this trunk strip down and glue on six or more cross strips. Trim them so you will get big rings at the top and small ones at the bottom end. Glue the rings together and then add a strip on the inside that will give the trunk its curve.

The ears are big roughly triangular shapes with glue flaps.

The tail is a tightly wound cone with some ragged additions on the swishy end.

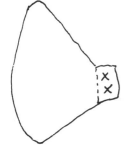

Tusks can also be made from cones.

This is a good place to look at a book and to decide if yours is an African or Indian elephant.

PAPER 'GATORS
from Cardboard Strips

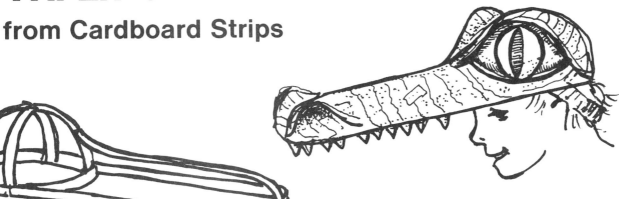

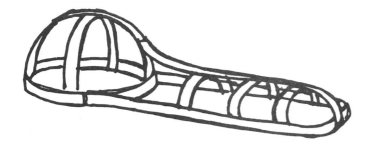

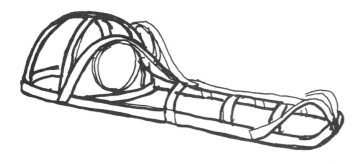

Start with a headband, then add the upper jaw with a long loop and a support on top.

Put more strips along the jaw to give strength and develop the shape.

The eyes start with two strips that loop up to make the eye sockets. Shorter strips make the nostrils. The eyes are rings or cutouts with drawn or painted decoration.

The teeth are cones made from grocery bag paper, and the covering is paper skin.

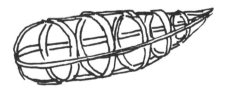

Ready to try something big? How about Moby Dick? Start with a cardboard strip profile to get the size and shape. It's like drawing in the air.

Light cardboard will do, but be sure the grain is right.

The next step is to fit a strip around his tummy to get an idea of how he will look when he gets filled out. You will need 6 to 8 strips to go around him like ribs.

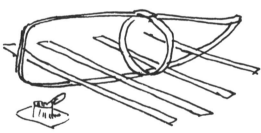

Glue the ribs to the bottom line of the profile, then curve them around and glue them together at the top.

Now run strips from the head to the tail along the sides to add strength and further develop the whale's shape.

Here Comes Trouble —

How do you wrap a flat strip around the tail end of your whale?

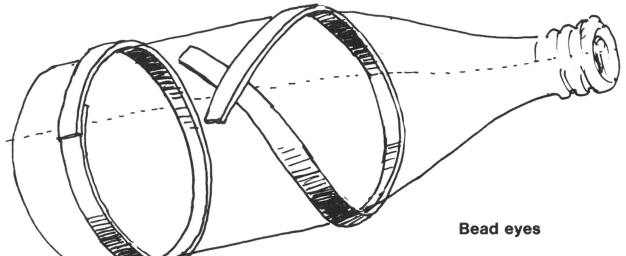

I've used a bottle to show you the answer. On the round part of the bottle the rings are simple — but when the shape changes to more of a cone, the rings have to be distorted to fit the changing surface. (It might be a good idea to do your own experiments with a bottle before you finish your whale.)

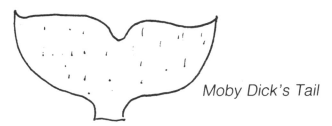

Moby Dick's Tail

The tail is flat, so you can cut it out of cardboard. It fits onto the body horizontally — not like a fish, whose tail is vertical.

Bead eyes

You can make great eyes with a bead and folded strips of paper for lids.

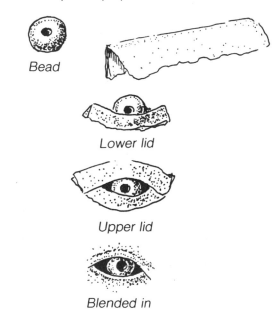

Bead

Lower lid

Upper lid

Blended in

The folded edge gives you the firm line around the eye, while the torn edge blends into the whale's body.

Put the lower lid on first and use a little more glue to make the lids quite flexible.

These eyes work on other creatures too.

Once again, the library is a good place to find pictures and stories about whales.

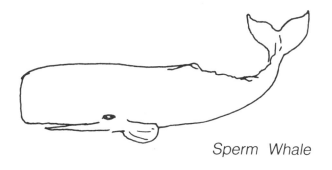

Sperm Whale

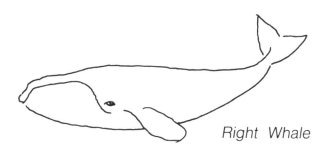

Right Whale

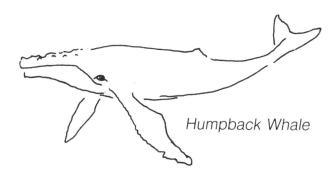

Humpback Whale

Killer Whale

Looking at whale pictures, you will see that whales come in many different shapes and sizes.

Here is a flipper for a sperm whale, like Moby Dick. It is small and roundish.

Flippers and flukes can be cut from cardboard and stuck on with torn paper strips.

Finishing Your Whale

You can make your models very large. If you had the time, energy, materials, and space, you could make them life-size. The bigger you make them, the more care should go into the framework.

If you do a really good job on the understructure, you will find the finishing goes faster and ends up better.

To make your frames tougher, you can paint them with any kind of waterproof paint. Then the wet pieces won't soak them.

To smooth out hollows on the skin, put wads of toilet paper blubber in the low spots and cover them with torn paper patches.

See Paper Skins for details (page 10).

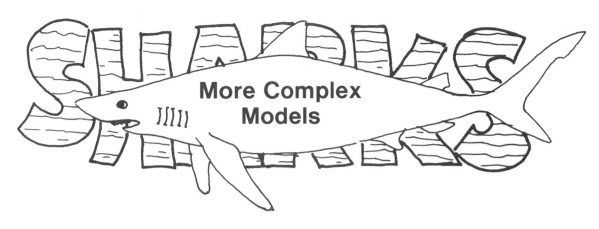

More Complex Models

The shark has a very well defined profile, as any scuba diver will tell you. But when we start to make models of sharks, we run into special problems that need new methods.

There are places on the shark where he has sharp edges, and these are hard to make with flat strips of cardboard. The alternative is to cut out a silhouette profile of the whole body. Include the tail but not the front fins. Use sturdy cardboard, and when you have it cut out, bend the body and tail into a lifelike curve that will make him seem alive and moving.

The next step is to make another profile. This time it is from the top, just as if you were looking directly down on him. Start by tracing the curve of the first profile onto another piece of cardboard. Use it as a center line to draw the top view — from the tip of his nose to the end of his body. (You don't need to include the tail on this one.)

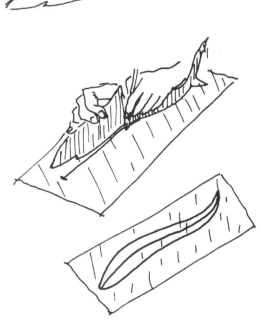

The next trick is to get the two halves of the top profile glued to the body.

You will need a lot of little paper tabs or hinges along the inside edge of each half.

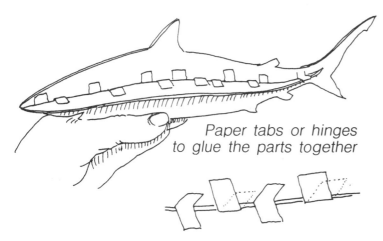

Paper tabs or hinges to glue the parts together

A very good trick is to glue half of the hinges on the top side edge and the others on the bottom. Then fold them in opposite directions before gluing them to the body — top flaps down, bottoms up. This gives you a tighter, stronger joint.

When you have all the flaps on the two side profiles, start at the nose and stick one of the two sides on. Take your time and keep pressure on them until the glue has set.

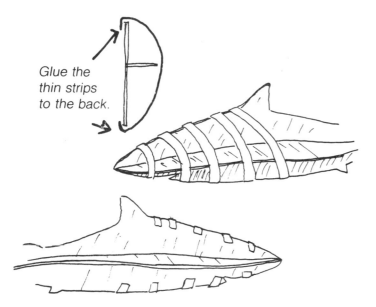

Glue the thin strips to the back.

The two profiles help you make a natural body shape.

Use thin cardboard strips to fill out the body shape. Keep it round and sharklike —glue the ends on the backside just like the tab/hinges.

Put ribs of thin cardboard on both sides until the shape is well defined. Then add cardboard strips, just like planks on a small boat. Bend them over the ribs and trim them so they do not overlay anywhere.

You don't have to cover every bit of the shark — but the better the plank job, the easier it will be to get a smooth finish.

General shape of the pectoral fins. "X" folds up for glue.

Sharks have very large pectoral fins that join the body at the widest point — slightly ahead of the dorsal fin and behind the five breathing vents.

Finish your shark with a final covering of paper strips, then spackle and paint. For more details on finishing see pages 12, 122.

UNDERSEA DIORAMAS

Dioramas are a really great way to make many classroom assignments come to life. The undersea scene is a good example. Dioramas can be made by individuals and they also work well as group projects. The library will give you a lot of picture books for ideas and examples.

Start with a big cardboard carton with a hole cut in one side which becomes a viewing port. The stage is now set for all kinds of creativity. The possibilities for dramatic adventures are so great with dioramas that you may want to suspend your characters on transparent threads and turn your project into a puppet theater.

I once survived a dreadfully dull high school English class by simply building a model of one of the scenes in "The Lady of the Lake." As a matter of fact I don't think I ever read the poem very carefully, but I think I got a "C" and I quite enjoyed building the model.

Reefs, Cliffs, Rocks, and Secret Supports for Fish

Very realistic rocks and undersea cliffs or reefs can be made from one or more pieces of crumpled GBP.* Glue their edges down to the floor and/or sides of your diorama. As you glue, keep shaping your structure to get the form you want. You can always add on or tear off if it isn't quite right. You may choose to leave your rocks their original GBP* color; however, a few patches of other colors here and there will give the effect of colorful coral and sea growths. Then, too, you might think about the grasses that grow under the sea.

CAVES can be easily made by tearing jagged holes in undersea cliffs or you can form them by wrinkling and folding the paper to form a very natural-looking cave.

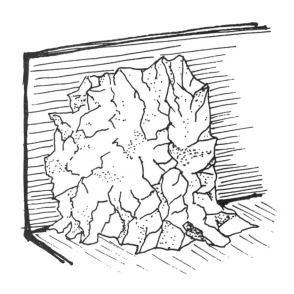

TECHNICAL NOTE For years I searched for something that would look just like rocks. At last I've found the perfect answer: ROCKS.

FISH THAT REALLY STAND OUT The trick here is to cut your fish from lightweight paper. Color them the way you want them to appear, then mount them on little strips of stiff paper that can be hidden behind the fishes' bodies. Another good trick is to place fish in among the grasses and weeds where they can be skillfully attached to bits of vegetation without its becoming obvious to the viewers.

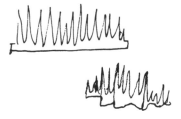

Seaweeds and Sea Grass Cut out strips of sea grass, then shape them in natural forms. Some fish swim in this grass.

* Grocery Bag Paper

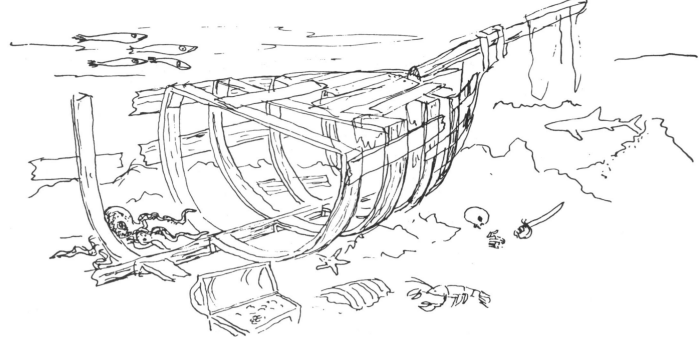

Shipwreck Construction

A simple way to build a wrecked ship is to start with a section of keel and the stem (bow). You can look at a picture of any ship and get a good idea of what the keel should look like. Cut it out of cardboard, then make some cardboard ribs. I generally make them about one cm (or a quarter of an inch) wide. They don't have to be exact. But you should be careful to see that the paper grain is running the short way, across the strips, so that they will bend into nice graceful shiplike curves.

You don't need a great many ribs. After all, this is a wreck. They should be set in pairs on each side of the keel. Curve them up to establish the shape you like and then add a few planks, also cut with a cross grain. These planks will keep the ribs in place and let you have fun shaping your ship and creating secret spaces inside.

Ribs are just cardboard strips. Check that the grain is going the right way.

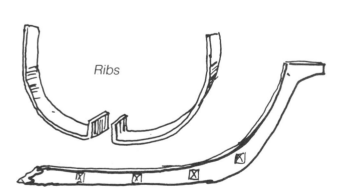

Ribs

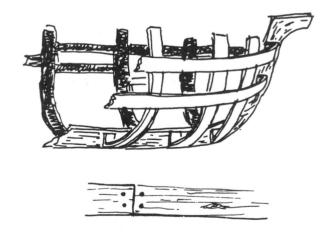

🗵 *Ribs join here.*

A piece of plank

A few fine pen lines can put realistic wood grains on your timbers. Round dots do well as bolts and nailheads.

Divers

THE DIVER'S BODY can be made with twisties and wads. The hands are paper mittens that attach at the wrists.

His feet are big and glumpy because they have weights in them to keep him from tipping over.

THE DIVER'S BELT

The diver's weight belt can be a strip for the belt and lead weights made from cardboard.

The helmet is the tricky part.

THE HELMET was formed in two halves over a small plastic ball. Wrap your ball in plastic or aluminum foil and make one half at a time. Build up the parts with two or three layers of glued paper bits. Keep the bits small and be sure they are torn, not cut. When you make the halves don't go crazy trying to get them to have exact edges. Make them a bit more than halfway and then trim them to fit together around the ball.

You can draw on the various details or you can cut them out and go wild gluing them on. If you choose to go the cutout route, it's a good idea to do the cutting out and gluing before you glue the halves together.

Basic Parts to the "Hard Hat" Helmet

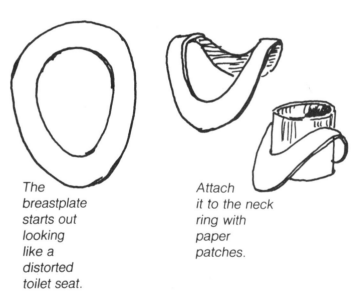

The breastplate starts out looking like a distorted toilet seat.

Attach it to the neck ring with paper patches.

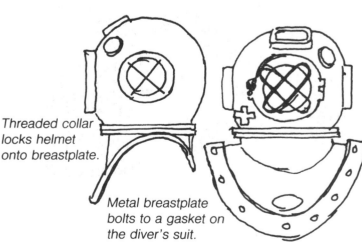

Threaded collar locks helmet onto breastplate.

Metal breastplate bolts to a gasket on the diver's suit.

Frogpersons

Frogpersons can be made like Bendinis or Twisties.

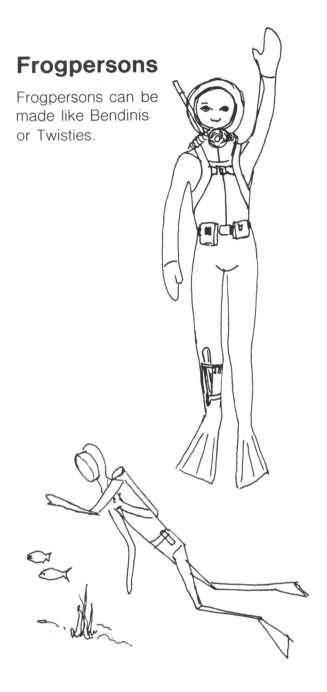

Building an environment for your diver can be wild.

Face Mask

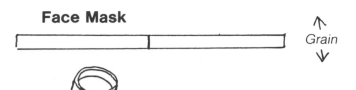

Wind up the mask until the end of your strip comes to the line. Then glue it together and glue it to your diver.

Tank

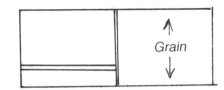

Do the same thing with the air tank and put it on your diver's back. Pipe cleaners or string can be used for the air hose. A wooden bead in the end of the air tank makes it look real.

Roll up a small tube for the snorkel. Cardboard weights on a paper belt

A snap fastener makes a super regulator.

 A wooden bead in the end of the air tank adds realism.

Pipe cleaners or string can be used for hoses.

125

BIG REX
An Oldie but a Goodie

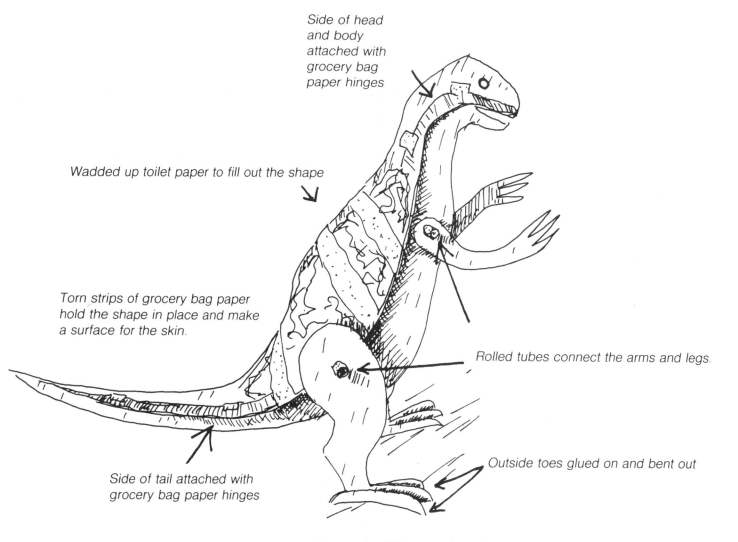

Side of head and body attached with grocery bag paper hinges

Wadded up toilet paper to fill out the shape

Torn strips of grocery bag paper hold the shape in place and make a surface for the skin.

Rolled tubes connect the arms and legs.

Side of tail attached with grocery bag paper hinges

Outside toes glued on and bent out

When you add the side patterns to the body profile you have a "3-D" outline that shows you how much padding is needed. Wad up toilet paper and stick it in place with torn strips of grocery bag paper glued to the profiles.

Do the body and head first, then the arms and legs. The rolled-up tubes make it easy to position the arms and legs.

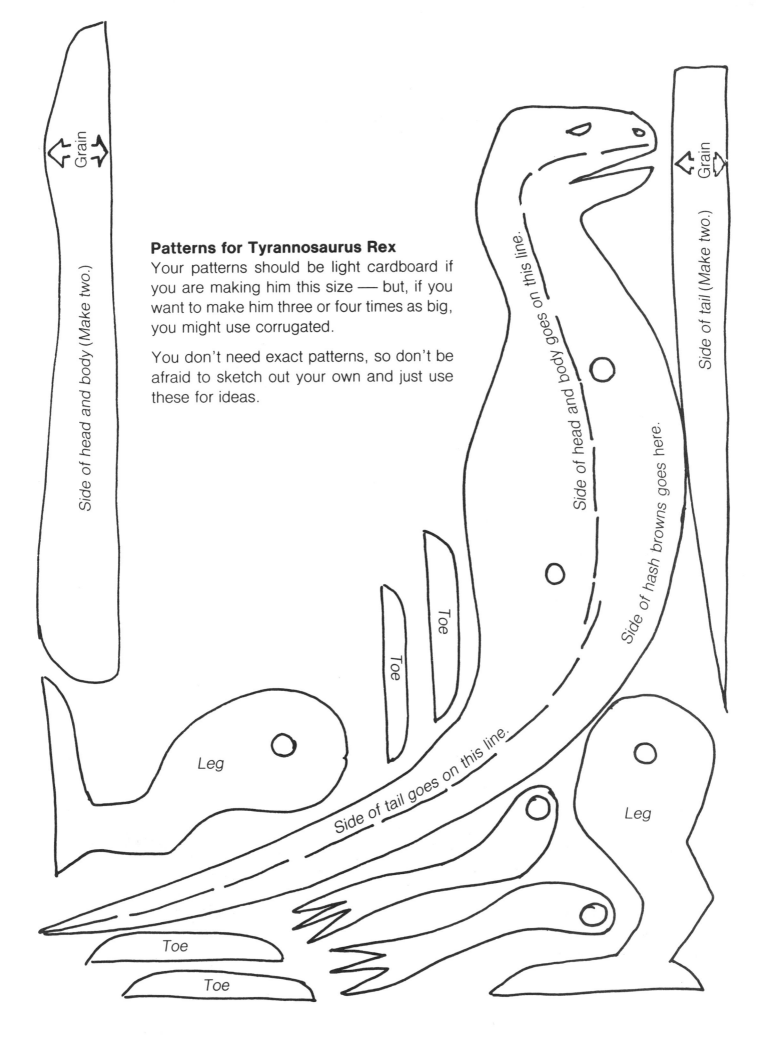

Patterns for Tyrannosaurus Rex

Your patterns should be light cardboard if you are making him this size — but, if you want to make him three or four times as big, you might use corrugated.

You don't need exact patterns, so don't be afraid to sketch out your own and just use these for ideas.

Side of head and body (Make two.)

Grain

Grain

Side of tail (Make two.)

Side of head and body goes on this line.

Side of head and body goes here.

Side of hash browns goes here.

Side of tail goes on this line.

Toe

Toe

Leg

Leg

Toe

Toe

INDOOR BOOMERANGS

This Is One Idea You Can't Throw Away.

Trace this pattern or — better still — create one of your own. Then cut out a boomerang from cardboard. The shape isn't really critical.

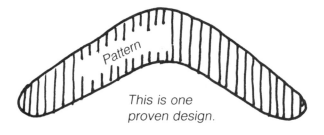

Pattern

This is one proven design.

The next step is important. You need to shape it slightly rounded (like a frisbee); that's what makes it fly.

Bird's-eye view of a launch

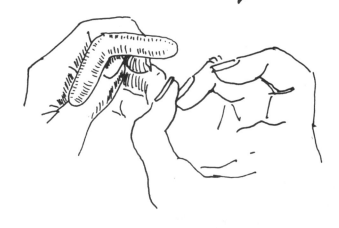

If you cut it in two, the cut edge would look like this.

You don't need a lot of curve, and you want the edges to lie flat on the desk when you lay it down.

The "Two-Handed Flick" method for launching. *Curve side up*

PUPPETS

Puppets can do things that people can't. Puppets can fly, they can fight dragons, they can do all kinds of outrageous things that kids could never get away with. They can also talk back and say things that kids can't say.

Puppets have always been a way to experience ideas and feelings that are hard to express.

For lots of kids, puppets can be lifesavers.

With puppets you can have great fun acting out simple nursery rhymes and fairy tales. Can you imagine Boffo as Prince Charming and the talking bird as Cinderella? Who do you think would make a good witch?

How about doing some stories of your own? The Bendinis could have some great adventures with cars or ships in a castle or in a magic tree stump. They might even live in a space station in one of the outer galaxies, or perhaps they could settle an undersea colony.

TALKING BIRD PUPPETS

You will need a stick about 20 cm. long and about 5 mm. in diameter. Glue (1) the inside beak firmly to the end of this stick.

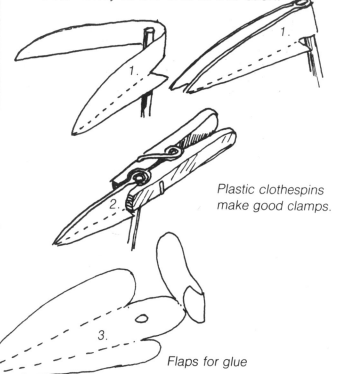

Plastic clothespins make good clamps.

Flaps for glue

Slip the stick through the hole in (2) the head and beak, and use those flaps to glue the two parts together.

Fold the sides of the beak up to meet at the center and use a small paper hinge to hold them.

Then glue along the ridge.

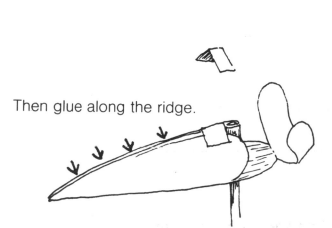

Finally — bring the back flaps forward and glue them to the beak.

Top view

Score beak and shape it into a shallow "V." Attach string with paper hinges covered with glue.

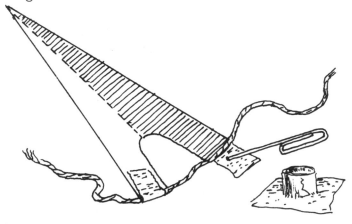

To operate smoothly, the lower beak must hang loosely.

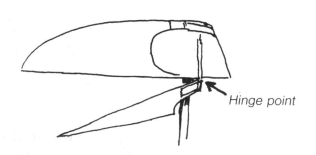

Hinge point

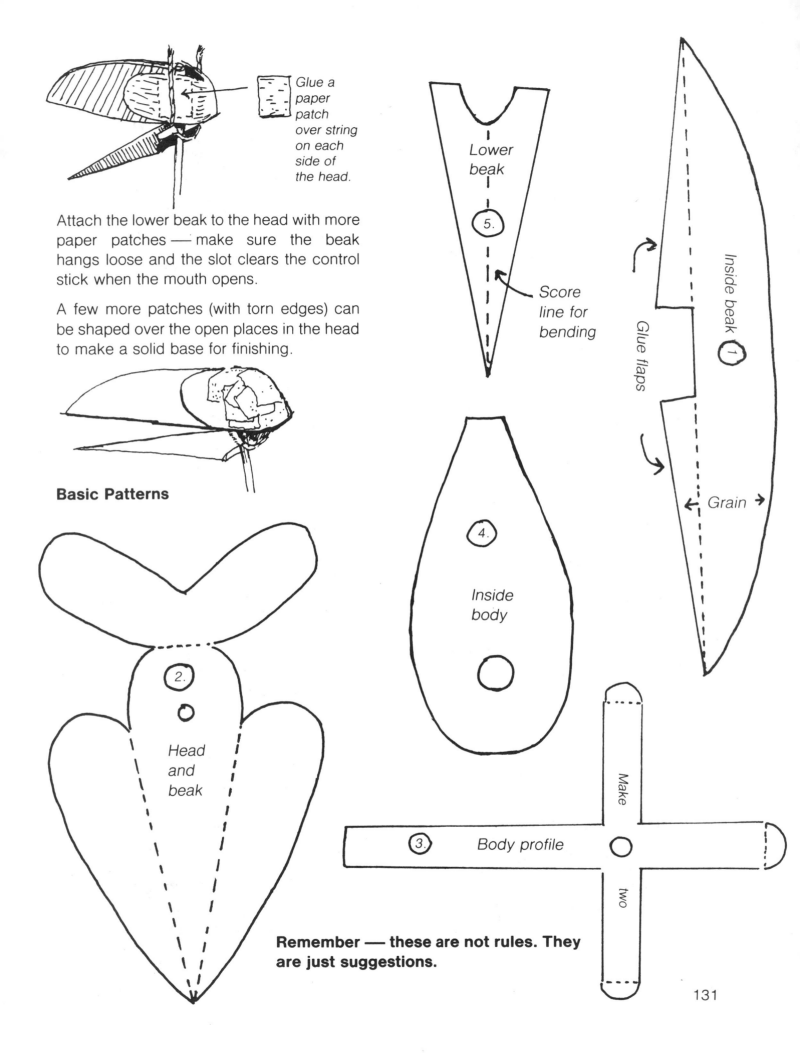

Glue a paper patch over string on each side of the head.

Attach the lower beak to the head with more paper patches — make sure the beak hangs loose and the slot clears the control stick when the mouth opens.

A few more patches (with torn edges) can be shaped over the open places in the head to make a solid base for finishing.

Basic Patterns

Head and beak

②

Lower beak

⑤

Score line for bending

Inside beak ①

Glue flaps

Grain

Inside body

④

Body profile ③

Make two

Remember — these are not rules. They are just suggestions.

131

1. Glue the top leg of one of the profiles to the fat end of the inside body piece.

2. When that's set, bring the long end around and stick it on to the other end (that's the tail).

3. Glue the two short arms to the underside of the body.

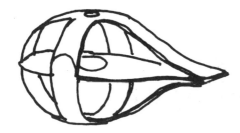

4. Glue the other profile on the underside — you should get something like this.

Cover the frame with strips of paper to round out your bird.

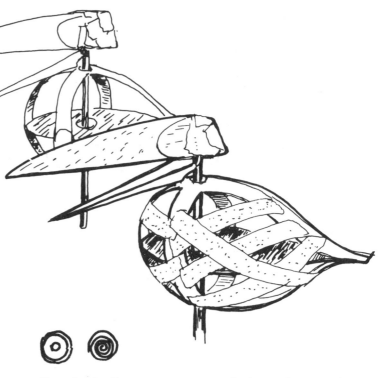

Beads, buttons, or paper spirals make good eyes.

When your shape is well established, you can use real or paper feathers. Start back at the tail and just glue the front ends. Put them on like shingles.

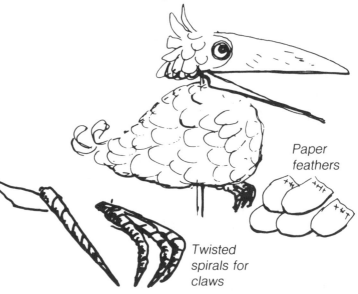

Paper feathers

Twisted spirals for claws

Grocery bags work fine for claws — and you really only need three claws to get the desired effect.

COW PUPPETS

This little cow's body is made from two spheres, one in front and one in back. The spheres are joined along the backbone and on the belly with a strip down each side.

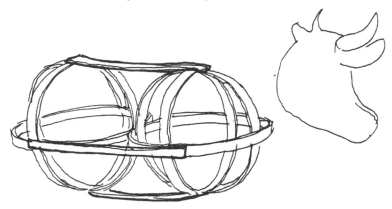

If you are careful to line up the connecting strips with the strips in the spheres, your work will be easier and your cow stronger. It also helps you to keep track of the top, bottom, and sides.

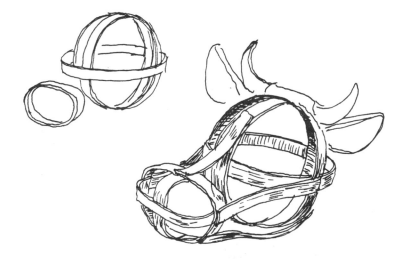

Start the head with a sphere and a smaller ring for the muzzle (mouth). Attach the muzzle with five strips — center forehead — each side — and two more at the edge of the jaw.

Start the covering with torn strips of grocery bags to set the shape — then follow the instructions in Paper Skins.

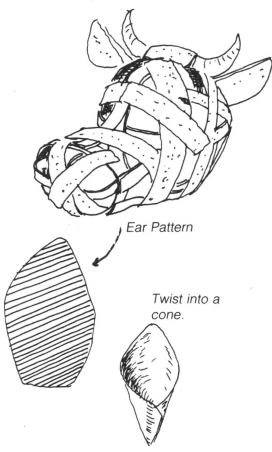

Ear Pattern

Twist into a cone.

Horns are tight rolls of grocery bag strips (torn).

Make two, bend them, and glue them together with a patch that sticks them onto the head.

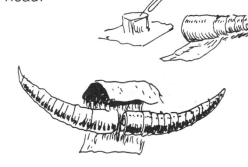

Give the horns a good coating of glue for strength.

Legs can be made from rope, cord, or a rolled-up strip of cloth.

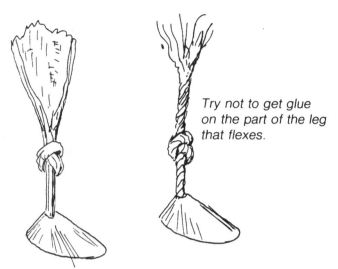

Try not to get glue on the part of the leg that flexes.

In either case, spread out the ends to give you a bigger area to glue onto the body.

Knots work fine for knees. You might say they are "knot-kneed."

Glue on the legs, neck, and tail with torn patches of grocery bag paper, and blend them in.

You can use the same stuff for the neck — make it long enough so she can graze.

Be generous with the paper patches that you put over the ends — we won't want her to come apart during the show.

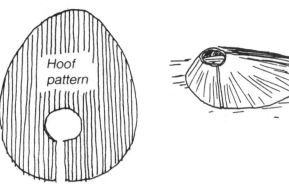

Hoof pattern

Cut out four cardboard hooves and use your fingers and/or the edge of a tool or a table to bend and shape them into cones. Then glue the overlapping ends.

Next: You need to glue the hooves to a bottom piece with a hole in it.

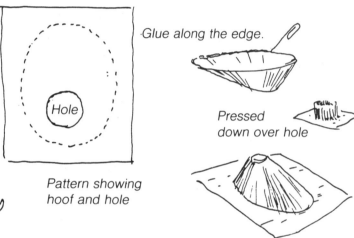

(Hole)

Pattern showing hoof and hole

Glue along the edge.

Pressed down over hole

Trim when the glue has set.

You may find it easier to cut the hole before you glue the two parts together — but you can just glue on a piece and cut out the hole — later.

The reason for this hole is to let you tie a knot in the end of the leg cord and slip it inside the hoof. And finally, cover the bottom of the hoof with one more piece of paper.

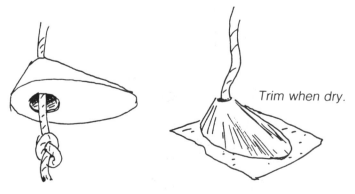

Trim when dry.

The udder has to be the right size for your cow, so start with a ring that fits her and then build up a dome shape with grocery bag strips that have been spread with glue.

The teats are just small rolls of grocery bag paper glued into holes in the udder.

Make them long enough so the ends can be glued to the cow's body.

Use the ends of the strips on the udder to glue the udder to the body.

The cow's tail can be made of cord, rope, twine, or yarn. The end is frayed out so it makes a good flyswatter.

The tail goes on top of the spine and makes a little ridge where it's glued on.

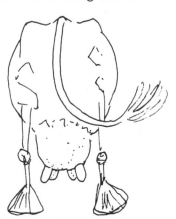

Controls *A simple two-stick cross made . . . to fit your hand*

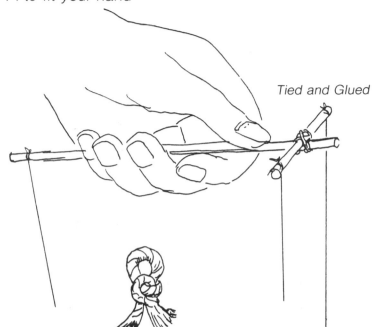

Tied and Glued

Control loops are made from string or thread — just make a small loop and tie a knot behind it — leave some short ends and fray them out for easy gluing.

The head loops are behind the ears.

Use glued paper patches to stick the loops firmly in place.

Cover the knot and the ends but leave the loop exposed.

For strings use thread or light fishline.

QUICK, EASY, AND PRACTICAL ENVELOPES
You Can Make Them from Writing Paper

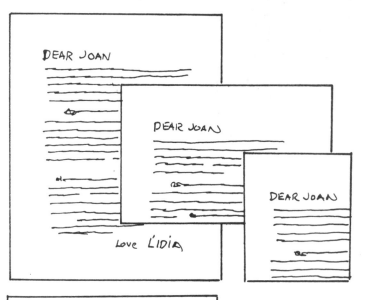

Fold your letter twice, once each way. Then lay it across another sheet. Fold the two sides around the letter, then fold up from the bottom. Finally, add some glue dots at the edges of the top flap and fold it over and squeeze.

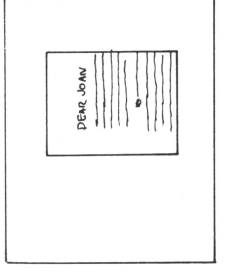

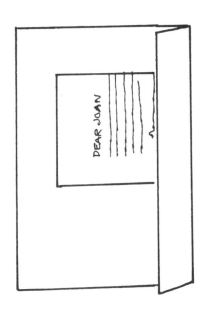

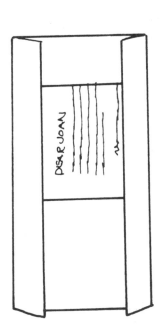

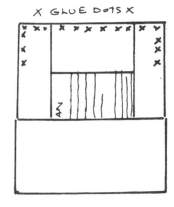

Of course, you still have to write that letter!

BOATS

TABLE-TOP TUGS

4. Bend the hull to its proper shape and glue the bottom to a flat piece of cardboard.

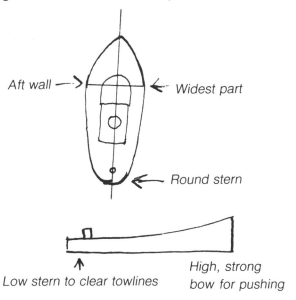

Aft wall → ← Widest part

← Round stern

↑ Low stern to clear towlines

High, strong bow for pushing

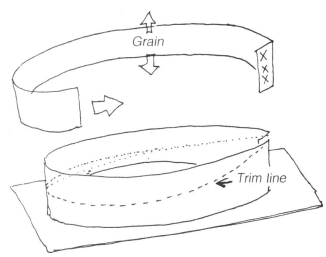

Grain

XXX → Trim line

1. Form the hull from a strip of cardboard. Make sure the grain is the right way.

2. Glue the flap "X" on the inside at the bow.

3. Trim the sides, high bow, low stern.

5. When the hull has been trimmed, put glue along the edge and lay on a piece for the deck. Take care about grain and be sure to press it down.

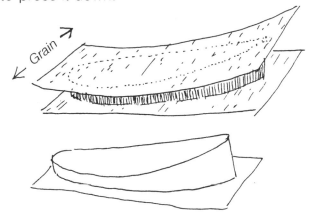

Grain

After the deck has set — trim it to match the hull and sand the edges smooth.

6. When the deck has set, cut out a "D" shaped opening for the pilothouse.

Cut a "D"-shaped opening for the pilothouse.

7. Measure the pilothouse opening with a small strip of scrap cardboard. Cut it so it is a snug fit.

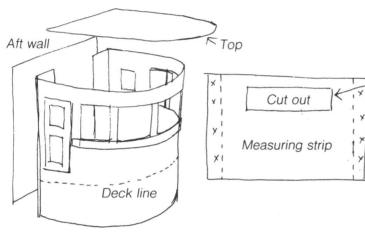

Aft wall

← Top

Deck line

Window opening

Cut out

Glue flaps added to each side

Measuring strip

8. Use your measuring strip to lay out your pilothouse. Add glue flaps to each end and try it in the hole in the deck. When you are satisfied, cut out the openings for the windows.

9. If you cut out one big panel for all the windows, you can make the strips that separate the windows from thin strips of cardboard glued on the inside.

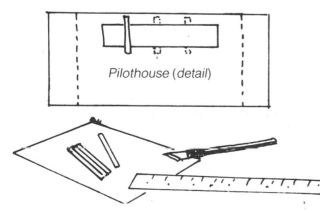

Pilothouse (detail)

10. The aft wall of the pilothouse is a strip just wide enough to fit the hole in the deck and as tall as the pilothouse.

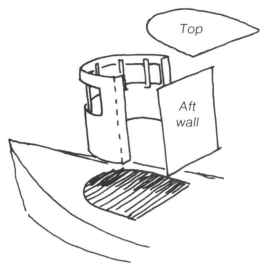

Top

Aft wall

The cabin top is the same shape as the pilothouse but a little larger, so it projects a bit on all sides.

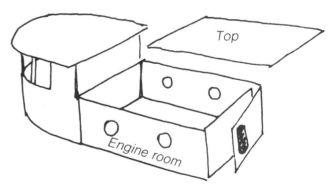

Top

Engine room

11. The engine room is a box made from a strip folded into five panels. The top fits up to the back of the pilothouse and projects on the other side.

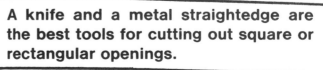

A knife and a metal straightedge are the best tools for cutting out square or rectangular openings.

The smokestack is made from a tube that you make by winding paper or cardboard to the right size.

If you want, you can wrap another hull skin around your tug.

The double hull means more strength plus a low rail that adds realism.

Make a hole near the stern to fit a tightly wound paper tube for your towlines. Put glue in the bottom of the hole and at the deck.

To cut the tube at an angle, prop up one side and slide a pencil around it flat on the table to mark where to cut.

Details

These are just a few suggestions — let your imagination go to work; this can be the best part.

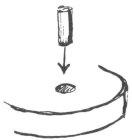

Running lights (port red, starboard green) go on top of the pilothouses.

Smooth any rough edges with sandpaper — emery boards work very well — after all, cardboard is made of wood fibers so it works like wood.

Use any kind of paint or markers for detailing. But — if you use water-soluble colors, add a final coat of some protective finish.

Bow bumper can be made from string or cloth or a wad of paper.

Rub rails and other details can be made from thin cardboard strips.

Tugs use dories or rowboats for lifeboats.

For pictures and details of tugs and lots of harbor stuff, check your library.

Make tires from a stack of "O" shapes. Tires protect the tugboat from banging against the wharf. The easy way to cut out the centers — cut through the tire; then when you glue several together, put each cut over the solid part of the one next to it.

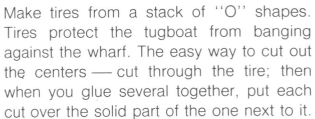

PILGRIMS, PIRATES, AND CHRISTOPHER COLUMBUS . . .

They All Sailed in Funny Little Ships, Much like This One.

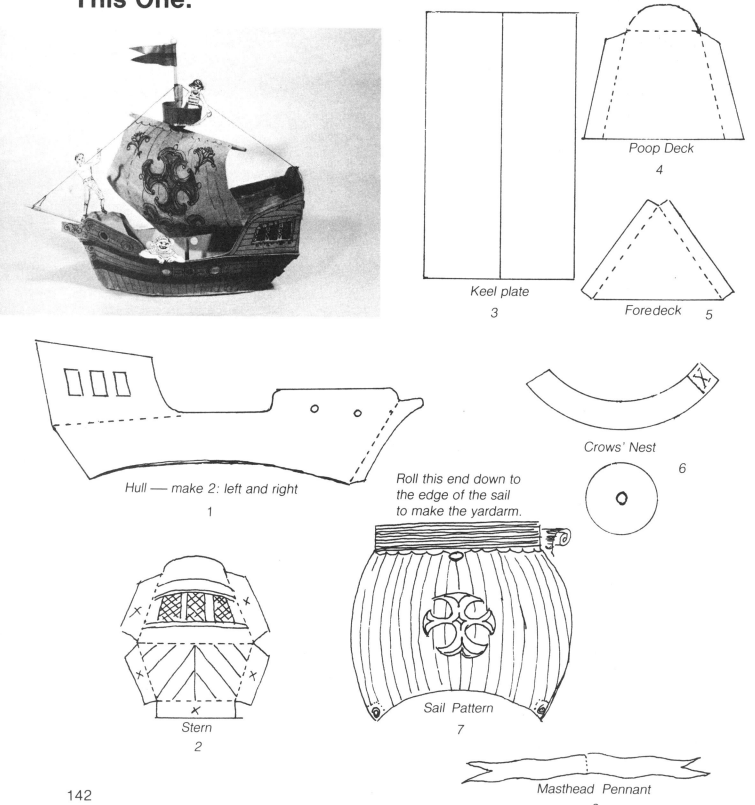

Keel plate
3

Poop Deck
4

Foredeck
5

Hull — make 2: left and right
1

Crows' Nest
6

Roll this end down to the edge of the sail to make the yardarm.

Sail Pattern
7

Stern
2

Masthead Pennant
8

Start by making the two sides of the hull — score along the dotted lines and glue the two sides together at the stem.

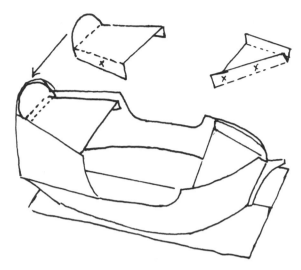

Cut out the stern (2) and carefully score all the dotted lines — make a keel plate (3) 4 cm x 7 cm with a 7 cm center line and mount the stern on center at one end.

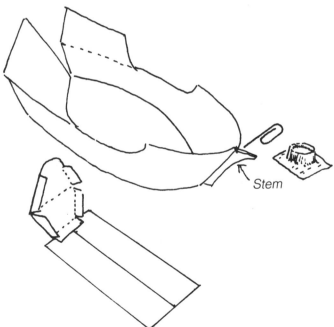

Stem

Glue the hull to the stern and then set it up on the keel line — glue it in place with dots of glue on the inside edge.

Cut out and score the two decks (4 and 5) (note how some of the glue flaps fold up while others fold down).

Your mast can be made from paper (by rolling) or wood — the bamboo skewers that come from Oriental shops work very well. A toothpick makes a good bowsprit.

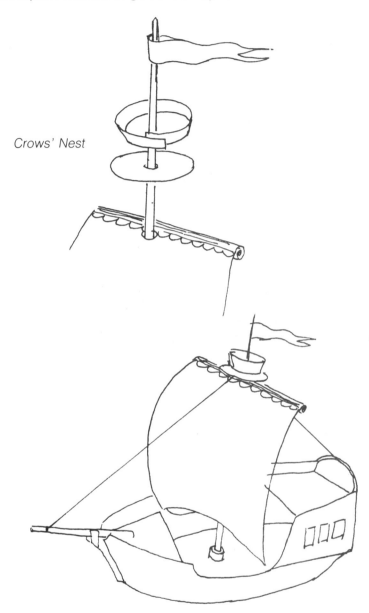

Crows' Nest

Make the mast stock from a roll of paper fitted around the mast.

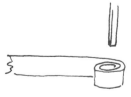

Adding details and decorations can be great fun — if you need ideas, try the library.

143

More Idea Starters

Tiny cannons can be just tubes sticking out of gunports.

Larger guns are fun to build from paper tubes with cardboard bases.

The anchor can be cut from three layers of cardboard with spade-shaped flukes and the stock added.

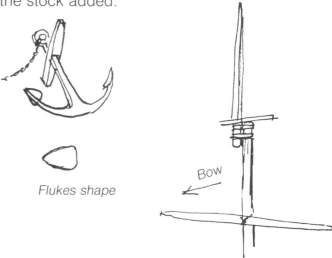

Flukes shape

Bow

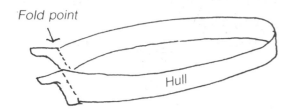

Fold point

Hull

The two sides of the stem. Fold at the hull so they can be glued together flat, to make one strong stem unit.

The bow must be very strong to support the bowsprit and the sails.

Bowsprit — *rolled paper straps*

Tall masts are made in two or three sections with the upper portion lashed to the front of the lower.

Yardarms for very small ships can be made from toothpicks.

Yardarms can be tied on with thread to match the rest of your rigging.

Three common sail shapes

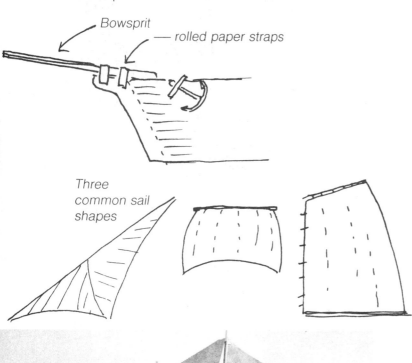

Warning to Shipbuilders

Watch out for Bendini pirates. They are always waiting to take over any unguarded ships.

THE TEACHERS' ANNEX

Visitors Welcome

One of the frustrating things about doing a book like this is that I don't have a chance to meet the reader face to face to talk about the things that mutually interest us and answer questions. It's like leaving a message in the oak tree. I just hope it says enough without being too confusing.

I do have a few other thoughts I want to share with you, and I have stuck them at the back so they would not get in the way of people who just wanted to make stuff without thinking about it.

Location photos by Bob Odell

What This Book Is All About

This book is an invitation to exploration and invention. It is an excursion into alternatives. It is meant to open the door to a thousand ways to create the things that excite you. It is also an invitation to try things without the fear of failure.

There are two factors that help this happen. First, the materials are cheap and widely available, so no one need worry about making costly mistakes. Secondly, the techniques are simple and require no special skills. In the long run they are "self-discovering." Most of the tricks or tools that I have presented here are things that just sort of turned up when I was trying to figure out how to make something with the stuff I had on hand.

145

Some Myths about Creativity

Both science and metaphysics tell us that we can create nothing. Even with a hydrogen bomb, all we can do is to rearrange the molecular furniture. Still we go on giving lip service to creativity. I suspect our nearest approach to creativity is making babies, but that's not what we are talking about in the classroom when we urge kids to be creative. As a matter of fact, we don't want kids to be creative. Creative kids are the ones who trip us up when we are wrong. They are the ones who figure out a totally different way to do things. They are the ones who give us an argument. They resist conformity . . . they are always trying to change a system that we have worked so hard to impose upon them.

No, let's not fool ourselves. It's tough to live with creativity, because it means constant change and continuing growth, and most of us are not up to that kind of challenge. On the other hand, if we can back off a bit from our well-established patterns and if we can tolerate a little disruption, we may give life to some fantastic growth in our students and in ourselves.

There is opportunity in art to experience real freedom, to kick off the fetters of convention. To go a little crazy and in the process save ourselves from going insane. It is a chance to experience the best of ourselves; perhaps that is the real creativity.

What Is Art and Who Are the Artists?

I believe that everything is art and everyone is an artist. No matter what the object is, it contains art. The discovery of art requires only that it is uncovered. I do not believe you can look closely at any of nature's works (and that includes the works of man) without discovering great artistic content. I think art is an essential element in the structure of the cosmos. The problem of discerning art is merely one of perception. Once we begin to sense how completely art surrounds us, we begin to see it. It's a matter of growth and expanding awareness.

I remember a discussion I once had with an aunt of mine about abstract art. She was a rural lady with absolutely no pretenses to culture, but she was a talented seamstress and a very sensitive person. She maintained that she just could not see what all the hoo-haw was about abstract art. In a way, she was saying that she expected art to tell a story in much the same way as the scenic illustrations did on the calendars she bought. I was trying to find some way to advance the case for abstract painting when my eyes fell

upon her hands resting in her lap on a blue and white paisley print dress that I knew she had made. I asked her, "Do you like that dress?" She looked at me as if I was having another of my frequent bouts of mindlessness. "Of course I like this dress. . . . I made it." "That's not what I mean . . . do you like the pattern in the fabric?" She looked down at the skirt and acknowledged that she did indeed like the pattern and was very fond of paisley prints. We talked for some time about the abstractness of the pattern, but I'm not sure I ever made my point. However, I do know that my aunt did appreciate abstract art even if she could not bring herself to realize it.

If you have ever marveled at a sunset . . . or a twisted bit of driftwood . . . if you have ever studied a snowflake or a cobweb, you know what art is.

Feeling Right about Being Wrong

If we are to encourage people to be creative, we must make sure that we have not paralyzed them with the fear of failure. Every artist, every scientist, and every inventor knows that there have to be thousands of wrong answers before there is one stunning discovery. Wrong answers are a very important part of discovery. It is those wrong answers that help you find the right direction to search out the final solutions.

When I was a kid, I once had a chance to take the wheel of a fishing boat and I was surprised that you didn't just point it toward where you wanted to go. You had to keep moving the wheel from port to starboard and back again, always passing across the direction you wanted to go. Actually, you hardly ever pointed the boat in that direction. Instead, you kept being wrong in one direction to overcome the error in the other, but eventually you got where you wanted to go.

Working with cheap materials and simple technologies gives kids a chance to try out new ideas, and, if they fail, to let those failures be part of the overall learning experience. If we do nothing more than make them feel that it's all right to make mistakes, we will do a lot toward making them happier and more productive individuals.

Accuracy

I'm one of those people who suffered most of a lifetime from a congenital inability to do anything with a high degree of accuracy. Thus, I have some very clear feelings about the subject.

The connection between accuracy and rightness and wrongness is obvious. Accuracy is a matter of more exactly determining how much righter or wronger you are.

In most instances it just isn't that critical. If you can get the car through the garage door without taking out one of the support posts, that's quite enough. Navigating our way through life depends more on general directions and many small corrections as needed. To be comfortable with our en-vironment requires that we have some over-all concept of where we are and what is going on, that we can see ourselves in relation to the things and events that surround us. In order to do this we must first have an overall view. We must be looking ahead to where things are not too clearly defined rather than concentrating on close-up details. Of course, there are times when people do need to focus sharply on the things close at hand, like when they are defusing a time bomb or performing a tricky neurosurgical nerve graft. But even these events can have meaning only in relation to a larger field.

If we can get the general picture, then we can focus on the details and provide the degree of accuracy that is needed.

Tracing, Copying, Modeling, and Replicating

Some teachers are shocked when I tell kids to trace. The realities are that one way to really understand a shape is to trace it. The tactile involvement coordinated with the eye provides a direct link between the subject and the brain. One of the places where this is now being demonstrated is in teaching some kids how to read and spell by having them trace the letters. Teachers are finding that the tracing process helps kids learn. I don't care how kids get the information they want, but I think it's up to us to help them rather than close them off from natural and effective methods that they will discover on their own if just given the chance.

Copying

When I went to school it was thought that copying would destroy imagination and creativity. What a bunch of hogwash! Imagination is grounded on the things we see and feel. Our whole conception of reality comes from our observations. We naturally copy the actions and activities that seem desirable to us. Copying is the way we learn to walk and talk and grow. So let's not be upset about copying. Copying things call excite you and introduce new ideas. If you get to a point where you can draw or paint or sculpt just like the artist you are copying, you will have found out a lot about yourself and about art and the process of learning.

Modeling

A great many of the projects in this book are a form of model building: the translation of some observable thing into a simulation of that thing . . . or a model. The process is an extension of the tracing thing. You have to become very aware of your subject to make a three-dimensional model of it.

Model building can give one a very intimate sense of the subject, and it also can open the doors to meaningful flights of fancy. I try to encourage students to take a nonreverent view of the subject and try not to replicate slavishly every nook and crevice. As a matter of fact, great fun can be had with making very unexpected changes, as in a racing turtle that has cheater slicks and multiple exhaust stacks emerging from his shell.

By not holding too close to the original, you will also save yourself from the paralyzing agony of endless detail and tight complicated measurements. Building a model that feels like the original is often a much better approach. If you can add some crazy touches . . . so much the better.

Replicating

There are times when you may want to make an accurate detailed model that actually duplicates the original. You can do it with paper and cardboard and in most instances quite effectively. But before you start, think about it carefully. Detailed accurate reproductions are demanding projects, and here again trying to get it right may come back to haunt you. When you make a free-form representational model you have much more room for originality. The reproduction imposes a form of tyranny that can be stifling.

FINALLY —

When I say "kids" I'm talking about you and me. I don't think that time erases "kidhood" — it's in every smile or chuckle, every silly notion or gentle touch to the very end of our lives.

Art helps little kids hang on to it and lets older kids nurture and develop their own precious sense of "kidness." It keeps us from becoming dull and stiff and uncomfortable. And it's kidness that keeps us young.

Art helps us endure the painful parts of our lives and celebrates the fun and fullness of our most vital moments.

Art helps us express those crazy sensitive parts that make us lovable. And it helps us move more softly, more gently through the universe. In the end, perhaps it will be art that will save us from ourselves.

Best wishes,

Jim Bottomley

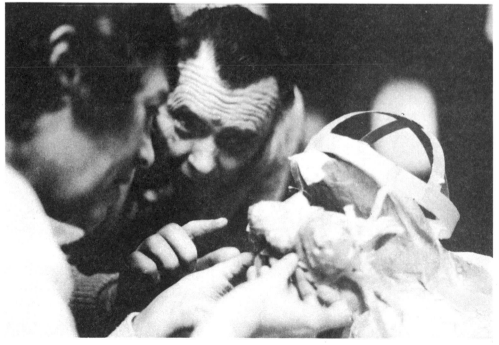

150